Abc of Harappan Script and Language

Sandirassegarane Gurunathan

BlueRose ONE.com
Stories Matter
NewDelhi • London

BLUEROSE PUBLISHERS
India | U.K.

BlueRose ONE
Stories Matter
NewDelhi • London

For permissions requests or inquiries regarding this publication, please contact:

BLUEROSE PUBLISHERS
www.BlueRoseONE.com
info@bluerosepublishers.com
+91 8882 898 898
+4407342408967

ISBN: 978-93-5989-063-0

Cover design: Muskan Sachdeva

First Edition: December 2023

Introduction

As the very title of the book suggested, you cannot expect detailed justifications for the interpretation of the Indus Script Signs and Inscriptions. They are available in sufficient extant in the main book,

Indus Script: Deciphering the Harappan Language and Grammar
(A Schemata for Possible Phonemes and Their Derivational Methodology)

The real purpose of this book is only to introduce the lay readers to the decipherment of the Indus Script achieved in the above publication, by way of ***collecting relevant excerpts***.

0.02 The Roman transliteration of Harappan words and texts proceeds as indicated below.

<u>**Short Vowels**</u>: ***a*** as in **'and'**, **i** as in **'bit'**, ***u*** as in **'put'**, ***e*** as in **'end'**, ***o*** as in **'toll'** a bit shorter.

<u>**Long Vowels**</u>: ***ā*** as in **'father'**, ***ī*** as in **'meet'**, ***ū*** as in **'root'**, ***ē*** as in **'where'** a bit longer, ***ō*** as in **'more'** a bit longer.

<u>**Diphthong**</u>: **ai** as in **'like'**

*The word final **ai** is very weak; it is pronounced as a semi-diphthong* with a sound combination of **a**, **e** and **ai.**

<u>**Enunciative Vowel Sound**</u>:

Hard consonants **ka ca, ṭa, ta, pa, ṟa** are called plosives. They cannot end a word as pure consonant; hence they add an enunciative **u** with a very short **u** sound; **it** vanishes when followed by a word-initial vowel sound.

Coming to consonants, as usual in Indic Languages, they all occur with their inherent **a** sound.

<u>***Plosives***</u>:

velar **ka** as in **'wake',** palatal **ca** as in **'chill',** retroflex **ṭa** as in **'take',**

dental **ta** as in **'think'** without frication**,** labial **p** as in **'paper',** alveolar **ṟ** as in **'trill'** with rolling**,**

A dental sibilant **sa** in some way very similar to English dental fricative **'th'** in *'think'*.

Nasals:

velar **ṅa** as in **'singer',** palatal **ña** as in **'ginger',** retroflex **ṇa,** as in **'random'** with retroflexing tongue in pronouncing **nd**

dental **na** as in **'name',** labial **ma** as in **'mom',** alveolar **ṉa** as in **'neighl'** with some rolling **on n.**

Following the Proto-Dravidian scholars and researchers, I have decided to use the transliteration of both dental **na** and alveolar **ṉa** *alike* and use **na.**

Others:

Approximant: palatal **ya** as in **'year',** alveolar **la** as in **'late',** labial **va** as in **'vent',** retroflex **ḷa** as in **'million'** with some retroflexing of tongue**,**

Flip: alveolar **ra** as in **'ram',**

Fricative: retroflex **ḻa** as in **'azure, pleasure'** a bit stronger as in French or Russian**,** glottal **ĥa** (āytam in Tamil ஃ) as in **'loch'** a bit more emphatically.

The Four Major Dravidian Languages are referred in this book as **Ta** Tamil, **Ka** Kannada, **Te** Telugu, **Ma** Malayalam.

(1) alveolar stop (**Ta** **ற, Ka ಱ, Te ఱ, Ma റ**) is denoted as **ṟ**

(2) the retroflex fricative (**Ta ழ, Ka ೞ ,Te ఴ , Ma ഴ**) is denoted as **ḻ**

(3) the Glottal fricative (Ta ஃ) is denoted as **ĥ**

Dedicated to my beloved wife,
(late) **Sozhan Madevy,** ***M.A., B.Lit., B.Ed.***

1. Preamble

Paragraphs marked with triple hashes **'###'** *in bold contain* ***Guidelines*** *and other important* ***hypotheses, conventions*** *and* ***remarks.***

***Guideline 01*** *In the Indus Script, the direction of writing is mainly from* ***Right to Left****. However, the other styles of writing, namely,* ***left-to-right*** *and* ***Boustrophedon*** *(alternately in both directions) are also found in a very few inscriptions.*

***Guideline 02*** *As we introduce signs, we shall give each an* ***appellative name****, by which it would be referred to in this book.*

1.01 A few words about the concepts of **homonyms, homophones** and **synonyms,** which are indispensable for proper understanding of any decipherment efforts, are given below.

Words spelt alike but with different meanings are called ***homonyms****. The word* **'right'** *in the sense of 'correct' and* **'right'** *in the sense of 'right-hand side'* are homonyms:

He is ***right*** *in his opinion on Mutual Funds.*
Please turn ***right*** *to reach your destination.*

Similarly, **'left'** in the sense of *past tense of 'to leave' and* **'left'** *in the sense of 'left-hand side' are homonyms:*

Has your friend ***left*** *his office?*
The green villa on your ***left*** *is my house.*

Words spelt differently with different meanings, but with the same pronunciation such as ***'rite', 'write', 'right', 'wright'****, are called* ***homophones:***

As per our religious custom, there are several ***rites*** *to be performed on the 15th day of a person's death.*

He prefers to ***write*** *letters rather than sending emails.*

He is always on his ***right*** *path to achieve his goals.*

*He considers himself as a great play **wright**.*

Different words with same or similar meanings such as, *'true – real', 'say – tell', 'buy – purchase' etc.* are called ***synonyms.***

<u>Guideline 03</u> *In ancient scripts, a sign or symbol created for a particular word is **automatically extended** to apply to its **homonyms, homophones** and **synonyms**.*

*When extension is made mainly on the basis of **sound** rather than meaning, it is called **Rebus Principle.***

2. *Indus Script and Inscriptions*

At the very outset, I would like to explicitly declare my stand on such issues as to whether the Harappan inscriptions unearthed so far constitute a **writing system** or not, and whether the underlying language is **Dravidian** or otherwise.

I am going to adopt the scientific methodology of ***'formal theories'*** *used overtly in* Geometry and covertly in Theoretical Physics.

2.02 In the above circumstances, the **axioms** or **postulates** that I adopt regarding the **Indus Inscriptions** are:

(1) *The body* of *Indus Inscriptions constitute a* ***Writing System,*** *which we may call the* ***Indus Script.***

(2) *The Indus Script is a* ***created script,*** *but not an* ***evolved one.***

(3) *The Indus Script was created on the model of* ***Mesopotamian Cuneiform*** *and* ***Egyptian Hieroglyphic.***

(4) *The underlying language to be named as* **Harappan Language***, is Proto Dravidian, an earlier version of* ***Classical Tamil.***

2.03 We have assumed that the Indus Script was created based on the experiences of the Mesopotamia and Egypt, adopting the cuneiform and hieroglyphic scripts as ***motivating models.***

Though the Mesopotamian cuneiform and Egyptian hieroglyphics co-existed in the same period of history, they were not of the same ***genre;*** they were indeed miles apart. They differed fundamentally from each other.

For instance, the Egyptian hieroglyphic was basically *a consonantal script,* where vowels played *second fiddle*; however, it was partially alphabetical thus qualifying itself as the forerunner of

abjad (alphabet) type scripts like English and other European and West Asian Languages living or extinct.

The ancient Mesopotamian cuneiform used by the Sumerians and Akkadians, was syllabic in nature, almost a forerunner to ***abugida*** (alpha-syllabary *or* pseudo-alphabet) type scripts now used in South Asia.

Nonetheless, since both the scripts evolved from pictures, the picture signs called ***logograms*** continued to be used as an integral part of their writing system for a long time, in fact, till their extinction.

At the beginning of any writing system, concrete objects we meet in our day-to-day life were tried to be drawn as pictures and these pictures conveyed to the reader the meanings implied by them. They are called **sense-signs** or **word-signs** or technically **logograms**.

Even though we often talk about pictographic scripts, we do not have and in fact, we never had **a purely logographic script** or in popular terms, a ***pictographic*** script for any spoken language in the world.

For judicious usage of a script, it requires additional elements other than mere pictograms, such as alphabetic signs, phonograms, diacritics etc...

2.04 At this stage, we also introduce the following ***subject related postulates***:

- The direction of writing is mainly **from right to left.**
- The Indus Script treats **short** vowels **'i'** and **'e'** alike.
- The Indus Script treats **short** vowels **'u'** and **'o'** alike.
- The Indus Script treats **plosive** consonants, alveolar (**ṟ** ற) and retroflex (**ṭ** ட) alike.
- The Indus Script treats dental **n** (**ந**)**,** and labial **m** (ம) alike.
- The Indus Script treats **plosive** consonants, dental (**t** த) and dental sibilant (**s** ஸ) alike.

Let us also make some ***linguistic or etymological oriented postulates***, as well.

2.05 According to some recent DNA based genetic research studies carried out by a large group of top-ranking scientists in the field *vide* ***Early Indians*** by **Tony Joseph** dealing with *'The story of our Ancestors and where we came from'*, there was an ***Out of Africa humanoid migration*** into South Asia, and they have since been living as **two major groups** for the past 65,000 years.

The two major groups are (1) the **Ancestral North Indians** (in short **ANI**) with a culture based on Indo-Aryan languages and (2) the **Ancestral South Indians** (in short **ASI**) with a culture based on Dravidian languages.

In the above circumstances, we can make the following additional **postulates**:

- At the time of Harappan Civilization, the people of ***Gangetic Valley*** and other peripheral regions were using a language to be called **ANI-Language** which parented the **Proto Indo Aryan** family in South Asia.

- At the time of Harappan Civilization, the people of ***Deccan Plateau*** and other peripheral regions ***including Indus Valley*** were using a language to be called **ASI-Language** which parented the **Proto Dravidian** family, and **to which belonged the Harappan Language** as per our earlier postulate.

- Both the **ANI** and **ASI** languages were always on **lend-and-borrow** mode; they also freely and frequently **exchanged grammatical features** and other basic **linguistic structures.** They already had a **shared vocabulary,** a part of which has continued for over 4000 years in both the regions till date.

2.06 In spite of the fact that the inscriptions found in the Indus Valley are mostly in **ASI** language (we called it the **Harappan**

Language), we cannot rule out the possibility that a sizeable portion of Indus population could have very well been **ANI** from neighboring Gangetic Valley, ***cohabitating*** with the then majority **ASI** people living in that region.

They could have **also** produced some inscriptions in the Indus Script, though in a considerably small number, *in their **ANI language;** I think I have identified a few of such inscriptions.*

We can give two major reasons as to why the presence of **ANI** *(Ancient North Indian)* language in ***Indus Inscriptions*** is *very scanty*.

One major reason is that during the heydays of Harappan Civilization, the **ASI** (Ancient South Indian) people were the **ruling class** and the **ANI** people who were **the ruling class of Gangetic Valley**, was only a ***minority in Indus Valley***; they have subsequently become a majority in the Indus Valley region ***only in post-Harappan periods***.

The second major reason could ***probably*** be that the **ANI** people were *compulsively* ***illiterate by choice***. Like the Aryans belonging to Bactria Margiana_Archaeological_Complex (BMAC), the **ANI** people *hated any writing system* and they preferred Karṇaparamparā (कर्णपरम्परा) for literary communication. They were, indeed, **doyens** for the spread of **oral-traditional** knowledge **in the world.**

3. Harappan Signs

3.01 There is uniformity among the Indus Script Researchers that the Script is ***logo-syllabic*** in nature, that is to say, a combination of pictures called ***logograms*** and phonetic syllables called ***phonograms***.

Both Egyptian hieroglyphic and Mesopotamian cuneiform are logo-syllabic scripts. Usually, any logo-syllabic script is comprised of the following components:

(1) Iconic signs called *ideograms* or ***logograms.***
(2) Syllabic phonemes called ***phonetic syllables*** such as *ra, pen, ket; ā, lu, gal,*
(3) ***Determinatives*** (Generic, Semantic and Phonetic)

These points are covered in more detail in the ensuing chapters.

In the early stage of development, a writing system always begins with pictures of concrete objects and actions associated with them, such as *head, mouth, teeth, foot, eye, ear, nose, arm, hand, leg, knee, human, cattle, fish, snake, bird, tree,* suggestive representations of *crop, river, mountain, city, house, fort, temple, sun, moon, star etc.* and related motions like eat, walk, see, hear, smell, do, work, live, worship etc.

However, before examining some of these pictograms, we are going to take a little ***digression*** for ***sentimental reasons.***

3.02 It seems to be a universal ***unwritten law*** that every script or alphabet should begin with a sign sounding **'a'**.

The Egyptian script starts with the **'a'** sound or Glottal stop, which is considered as a consonant rather than a vowel and represented by their National Bird, 'vulture' as hieroglyph, namely,

.

The Mesopotamian cuneiform begins with the vowel **'a'** represented by Sumerian word for **'water'**,

namely, 𒀀

We know about later alphabets,

Greek begins with **'alpha'** (α), Hebrew with **'aleph'** א,

Arabic with **'alif'** ا, and Indic alphabets with the short vowel **'a'**: Assamese **অ**, Bengali **অ**, (Devanagari) Hindi, Konkani, Marathi, Nepalese etc. **अ**, Gujarati **અ,** Odisha **ଅ**, Punjabi **ਅ,** Sinhalese **අ**, Tamil **அ**, Telugu **అ**, Kannada **ಅ**, Malayalam **അ**,

"akara mutala eḻuttellām" **(அகர முதல எழுத்தெல்லாம்)**

The ancient Tamil ethical work of repute 'tirukkuṟal' (திருக்குறள்) declared in its very opening verse that ***all scripts begin with 'a'*** and the said verse[1] itself begins with the short vowel **'a'**.

"athāto brahma jijñāsā" (*अथातो ब्रह्म जिज्ञासा*) *'Now therefore the desire to know Brahman'* is the opening line of **Brahma Sutra**, a foremost Philosophical work of India; observe that the verse begins with **'a'**.

In the very first sutra itself, the ancient Tamil Grammar, Tolkāppiam (தொல்காப்பியம்) describes the Tamil alphabet as:

---

[1] அகர முதல எழுத்தெல்லாம் ஆதி
பகவன் முதற்றே உலகு.
திருவள்ளுவர் - குறள் 1

"akara mutal ṉakara iṟuvāy" (அகர முதல் னகர இறுவாய்...) (starting with **a** and ending with **ṉa...**)"

South Asia from time immemorial seems to be obsessed with *spirituality* or ***dharma*** and the Harappan word for dharma is **aṟam** (அறம்). As you can see, this word begins with **short** vowel **'a'.**

The Indus Valley scholars, intent to create a script to their language following the footsteps of the Egyptian and Mesopotamian writing systems then in vogue, searched for some ***tangible clues*** to ***choose a picture*** to represent their word for dharma, **aṟam** (அறம்), so that the same could be used both as a *logogram* with sound value **aṟam** (அறம்), and *phonetic syllable* **'a'** (அ).

Eventually they found their choice, namely, the basic fish sign:

Why this choice? Here is a plausible explanation.

The Egyptian Hieroglyphic was a consonantal script; in this script, there are signs only for consonants and the readers are expected to supply relevant vowel sounds from their knowledge of and experience with the spoken language.

For example, the word **aṟam** will simply be '**ṟm'** omitting the vowels; but **rm** meant **'fish'** in Egyptian.

Please see the extract from Gardiner's Egyptian Grammar reproduced below:

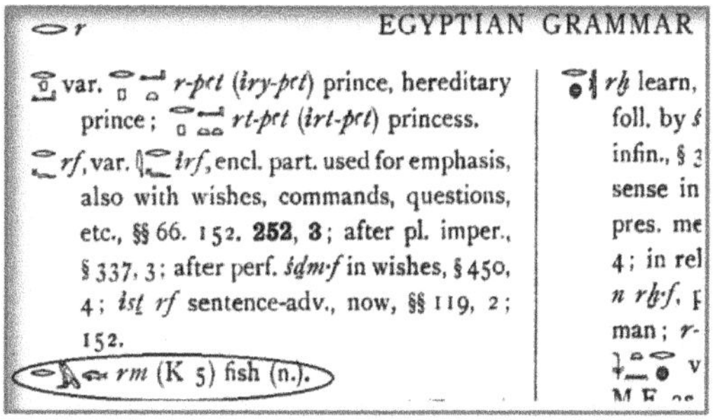

r EGYPTIAN GRAMMAR

var. *r-pˁt* (*iry-pˁt*) prince, hereditary prince; *rt-pˁt* (*irt-pˁt*) princess.

rf, var. *irf*, encl. part. used for emphasis, also with wishes, commands, questions, etc., §§ 66. 152. **252**, **3**; after pl. imper., § 337, 3; after perf. *sḏm·f* in wishes, § 450, 4; *ist rf* sentence-adv., now, §§ 119, 2; 152.

rm (K 5) fish (n.).

rḫ learn, foll. by *s* infin., § 3 sense in pres. me 4; in rel *n rḫ·f*, man; *r-*

*(Cited for illustration purpose from **Gardiner's Egyptian Grammar**)*

On the other hand, in archaic Sumerian, there is a pictogram depicting **fish** which serves, amongst others, as phonetic syllable **'a'** named **a_7** as well as glottal stop **a_4**

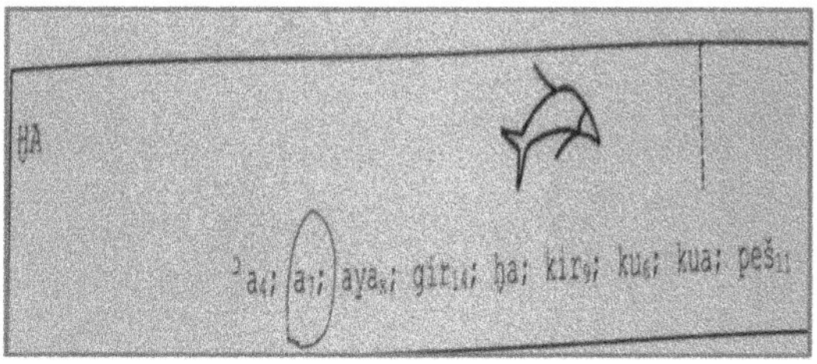

(Cited for illustration purpose from *Archaic Sumerian Pictographic Signs* ***by Ashur Cherry, Canada)***

The Indus Scholars, entrusted with the onerous duty of formulating a writing system to their language, have successfully created their **first logogram** with derived syllabic value:

 = logogram **aṟam (அறம்),** phonetic syllable ***'a'*(அ)**

Now we have our first entry to the Harappan G**lossary,** namely, 

4. *Other Vowels in the Indus Script*

4.01 In the previous chapter we saw that the basic fish sign could be adopted as the vowel sound **'a'** with logographic phonemic value ***aṟa / aṟam.***

The iconic value of this sign, namely, *mīṉ* - fish, as well as its Rebus value **'star'** became part of the phonetic schemata of the Indus Script.

	=	***aṟam*** (அறம்), short vowel **'a'** (அ),
		iconic value ***mīṉ,*** (மீன்) 'fish', 'star'

4.02 <u>**Modified Fish Sign for 'i':**</u>

Next to ***aṟam*** (அறம்) *'dharma'* comes the concept of <u>*royalty/divinity*</u>, **iṟai** (இறை) *'God / King'*. However, the committee felt that it was not necessary to find a sign to God / King after duly following a complicated exercise as in case of *dharma.*

At this point of discussion some members could have suggested that a sign to **irai** *may be created* by modifying the fish sign *already approved for 'dharma'* with the addition of a <u>***moustache,***</u> since moustache is an instance of Harappan grammatical upper-class **uyartiṇai,** (உயர்திணை); fish with moustache was chosen for **iṟai**, a word used for both God and King. We know that unlike prawn, fish doesn't have moustache as may be seen from the picture below:

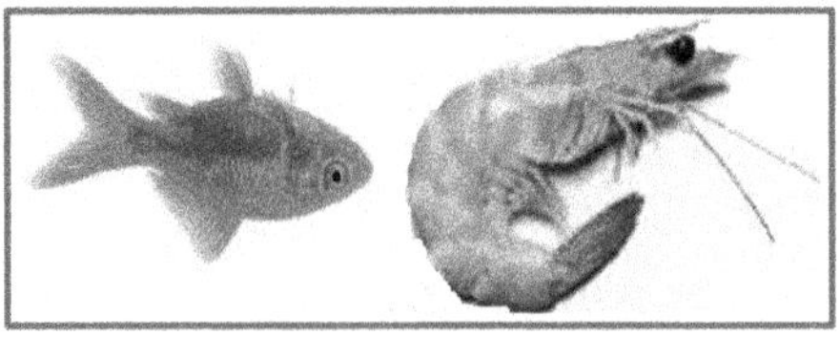

As such, fish sign modified with outward radial diacritic was chosen to represent the abstract concept of **iṟai** and the phonetic syllable for vowel sound 'i':

 = **logogram iṟai** (இறை) 'god, royalty'

Phonetic syllable **short vowel 'i',**

*This sign is also used to denote the short vowel '**e**' as we have already hypothesised that the Harappans treated short vowels '**I**' and '**e**' alike.*

 = **short vowel 'e'**

It is also interesting to note that the word for prawn is 'இறால் /எறால்' (**iṟāl / eṟāl)** *with the initial sound of 'i / '**e**'.*

4.03 <u>Modified Fish Sign for 'u'</u>

Next come the important concepts of ***'home', 'wealth' and 'possession'***. Since a person possessing wealth is considered to be entitled to wear **talakaṭṭu,** headgear, the basic fish sign was modified by addition of a cap, also implying 'roof'. 'Roof is associated with home / residence.

 = **short vowel 'u'**

uṭai (உடை)– dress, possession or wealth

uṟai (உறை)– home, residence

uṭu (உடு)– to wear, to dress, **star.**

*This sign is also used to denote the short vowel '**o**' as per our hypothesis.*

 = **short vowel 'o'**

4.04 Long vowels.

In the beginning, the long vowel **ā** was ***probably*** denoted by a double-fish sign:

 = **archaic** long vowel **' ā'** (ஆ)

There are a few rare inscriptions containing this double-fish sign; but in course of time, the double-fish sign gave way to:  literally meaning 'two fish'. Hence, I identify:

 = **long** vowel **' ā'** (ஆ)

This compound sign ***treated as a single entity*** also denotes the domestic animal of importance, **'cow'** or **'cattle'** as intrinsic value of the logogram:

 = cow, cattle

 = **ā,** (ஆ, மாடு, செல்வம், பொருள்) ***'cow, cattle, wealth, property'***

4.05 In earlier days the number of fingers on a hand was the ***highest number conceivable by Man in the beginning of his intelligent thinking.***

In those days, seven (7) was 'five + two' and eight was 'five + three' in Sumerian. In Roman numerals also, 7 is 5+2 in symbols **VII** where **V** is five and **II** is two**; and** 8 is 5+3 in symbols **VIII** where **V** is five and **III** is three.

In Harappan civilization, the base-number concept was extended first from (5) to eight (8) and later on to ten (10) , but 'five' was still **exclamatory 'ai'**(ஐ). Hence, the basic and important diphthong 'ai' was denoted by:

 = **diphthong** 'ai' (ஐ)

The logogram  **ai** (ஐ) also denotes **'elder', 'leader', 'father'** and leader's synonym **'head'.** Hence it is the sign for **talai** (தலை) *'head'* **in Indus Script.**

 = **talai** (தலை) *'head'*

4.06 Next, we consider the long vowels **'ē'** and **'ō'** which are closed ones in Dravidian Languages.

Greek had both closed and open 'e' and 'o': ***originally***, η (ēta) and ω (omega) were open while ε (epsilon) and o (omicron) were closed; but later on, they simply became ***long and short vowels***.

Open long '**ō**' is represented as '**au**' in French and similarly the basic Vedic mantra '**om**' is usually written as **'aum'** to emphasize the fact that the '**o**' involved is open, but not closed.

Since the long 'o' in Dravidian is **closed**, it is represented by **'ua'** (compare **uvaccan உவச்சன்** and **ōccan ஓச்சன்**; **uvakai** உவகை **okai** ஓகை)

 = **ō**

Word-initially,  has also been used as open 'o' written as **ɔ.** Only this sign is used in Harappan for **'om'** in divine invocations.

Similarly, Open long '**ē**' is represented as '**ai**' in French and by analogy, I assume that the combination '**ia**' could very well have denoted the long vowel **'ē'** (compare **ialāmai** இயலாமை and **ēlāmai** ஏலாமை of same meaning.**)**

 **= ē**

Word-initially  might have been used as open 'e'

From examination of various inscriptions with the help of ***Indus Script Analyser***, the long vowels **ī** and **ū** are represented tentatively as***:***

IIII = **ī** and

III = **ū;** *but this combo sign is also used as an alternative to the short vowel*  *exclusively for* **u** *sound, but not for* **o** *sound.*

In tabular form:

 = **ō** (long 'o' closed)

 = **Ɔ** (long 'o' open)

 = **ē** (long 'e' closed)

 = **Ɛ** (long 'e' open)

IIII = **ī**

III = **u** or **ū**

4.07 Phonetic Modifiers (Vowel modifier)

My intense research and deep analysis of Indus Inscriptions have ***given me an idea*** that unlike Mesopotamian Cuneiform or Egyptian Hieroglyph, the Indus Script had a **vowel modifier** which, when ***placed before a logogram*** modifies the first vowel sound from short to long and *vice versa*.

In my opinion, the Indus Script had at some early stage, two separate signs, one to lengthen short vowels into long ones  and the other to shorten the long vowels into short ones , but in course of time the Indus Valley scholars felt that the existence of two signs for this purpose was ***redundant*** and adopted a single sign. The sign is

4.08 Phonetic Modifiers (Consonant modifier)

There is another phonetic modifier of interest in Indus Script which is applicable to consonants, particularly the surds **(k, c, ṭ, t, p, ṟ)**; this *consonant modifier* is the fish sign with a dot:

If this modifier sign **is placed before a logogram**, the effect is to **modify a double surd into nasalised surd** and ***vice versa:***

-kk-	into	**-ṅk-**
-cc-	into	**-ñc-**
-ṭṭ-	into	**- ṇṭ-**
-tt-	into	**-nt-**
-pp-	into	**-mp-**

We can learn the above modifiers by judicially applying them to some concrete situations.

Let us now consider the famous logogram denoting 'palace', 'temple', 'fort':

 = **kōṭṭai** (கோட்டை) *'temple', 'palace', 'fort'*

However, this sign is also used as a **phonogram** with phonetic value **- ṭṭ-** (-ட்ட-) in *word-medial* position.

When the **logogram** is accompanied by one or more vowel / consonant modifiers **we get different sound effects:**

 = **koṭṭai** (கொட்டை)  modifies long **ō** into short **o**)

 = **kōṇṭai** (கோண்டை) ( modifies **ṭṭ** into **ṇṭ**)

 = **koṇṭai** (கொண்டை) (**ō** > **o**, then, **ṭṭ** > **ṇṭ**)

When both the modifiers are employed simultaneously, the consonant modifier should come first, followed by the vowel modifier as indicated below:

The combination  *is **not** attested anywhere in Indus inscriptions*

The following sign denotes 'fowl' **kō<u>l</u>i** (கோழி):

When phonetic modifier is added to this sign, the vowel value of the sign stands modified with short vowel o:

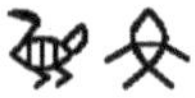 = **ko<u>l</u>i** (கொழி) *'flourish'*

5. Vocabulary building

5.01 The Mesopotamians had two methods to highlight portions of existing signs to produce words denoting the 'highlighted portions', namely *gunū* and *šeššig.*

Observe that in the Sumerian, the *'mouth portion'* of the already existing head sign is modified with a few more strokes to create a sign for mouth:

This method is called *highlighting by* ***gunū.***

The other method mentioned by us, namely, the ***šeššig*** method involves in hatching the portion to be highlighted. Hatchings are done by adding a few pictures of paddy crop in horizontal or curved position  .

 DA ('shoulder, side')

After adding *šeššig* hatching it becomes:

 A_2 ('arm')

We find instances of both methods of highlighting in the Indus Script. Further the Harappans have also devised **their own innovative methods**, which may be illustrated through the following example.

Recently I have come across a simple mind-bender game:

> "Read out the following, finding the **rebus** involved in the numeral portion: **023456789 lives forever".**

If you carefully observe the numeral portion, you'll find easily that there is ***no*** **'1'** in it. Hence, by using Rebus Principle, the number

023456789 is to be understood to mean **'No one'** and the whole expression is to be read as '**No one** lives forever'.

The innovative methods devised by the Indus scholars are in a way similar to the above mind game. Let us see an illustrative example. The pictogram for 'night, rain' in Archaic Sumerian is:

Motivated by the above, the Harappan Scholars have designed their own sign for ***'rain'*** taking into account the local conditions. In the South Asian region, rain *with wind* falls mainly in two slant directions depending on the two major monsoons, South-West and North-East:

 = **maḻai** (மழை), ***'rain'***

Considering the fact that the **strokes cover all sides and corners** around us, the content of this sign has also been semantically extended to denote **muḻu** (முழு), 'whole'.

In fact, both **maḻai** and **muḻu** are cognates from ***Egyptian point*** of view, if you observe them carefully, because they have only the *same set of consonants*, **m** & **ḻ** once you ignore the vowels as the Egyptians did.

 = **maḻai** (மழை) 'rain'; **'muḻu'** (முழு) 'whole, entire'

The Harappan scholars went ahead a step further to denote the concept **'edge'** by modifying the sign by ***removing*** one corner / edge stroke:

 = **nuni / muni / munai,** (நுனி / முனி/ முனை) 'edge'

I call this type of modification as ***'highlighting by omission'.***

The sign means, among others, *muni* which has a homonym **'muni'** (முனி) meaning **a rural deity**; hence by application of **Rebus Principle,** the value of the sign is extended to mean the rural deity **'muni';**

 = **muni** (முனி) *'rural deity **muni**'*

<u>This type of innovation is rampant in the Indus Script.</u>

5.02 The Egyptians had three different signs for mouth and lips:

 = **ra** 'mouth'

 = **sepet** 'upper lip with teeth', and

 = **sepetey** 'two lips with teeth'.

The Indus scholars have, for reasons only known to them, have adopted their mouth sign from the Egyptian hieroglyph, 'mouth with both lips' or 'two lips with teeth'. The adoption is of *geometrical caricature* nature:

 = **vāy** (வாய்) ***'mouth'*** in Indus Script.

This example amply proves that the Indus Scholars freely innovated on the Mesopotamian and Egyptian models to suit their own requirements. For example, the Indus Scholars have culled out a portion of their mouth-sign to denote tooth:

 = **pal_2** (பல்) ***'tooth'*** in Indus Script (observe that it is the *'upper denture'* in the mouth-sign). This is going to be a very important sign. You can liken it with the Egyptian hieroglyph***, 'upper lip with teeth'*** mentioned above.

At one stage in the development of the writing system, the Mesopotamians turned some of their signs 90^0 anti-clockwise ***to save horizontal space*** and the Harappans followed suit. The above sign became:

 = **pal_1** (பல்) 'tooth' among other meanings.

The word 'pal' has a homonym 'pal'(பல்) meaning 'many'. Since 'many' denotes plurality, the meaning of this versatile sign was extended to mean the plural particle **'ār'** (ஆர்) used mostly as **'honorific plural suffix'**. It is in this later sense that the sign is predominantly interpreted in this volume:

= **ār** (ஆர்) 'honorific plural particle' and also the plural suffix **kaḷ** (கள்)

5.03 Next, we may consider:

= **lu** *'man / person'* in early Sumerian

= *man / person* in Egyptian

Motivated by the Egyptian symbol, the Harappans devised their sign for man as:

= **mān, makan** (மான், மகன்) *'king, leader, man / son'* in Indus Script.

makan (மகன்) *'son'* is a transform of **mān** (மான்) as we are going to see in a forthcoming pages that a *long vowel splits itself into two short vowels; in the process, a euphonic consonant is added between the two split short vowels.*

mān (மான்) >>> **ma + an** >>> **ma + k + an** = **makan** *'man, son'*

= **āl, aṭi** (ஆள், அடி) *'person / slave/ servant'* in Indus Script.

Woman follows,

= **munus** *'woman'* in early Sumerian

 = **nebt** 'lady / *woman'* in Egyptian

If you carefully observe the Egyptian hieroglyph for woman, you will find that the sign carries two plaits on the back of the head. Motivated by this example, the Indus Scholars have caricatured adopted human sign with double plaits as *'woman'* in the Indus Script, *as usual in caricature mode,*

 = **āṭṭi,** (ஆட்டி) *'woman'* in Indus Script.

5.04 There are some more Sumerian pictographic signs which could have motivated the Indus Script. In this regard, we may cite the grain, hand which we have already met and some others:

 = **še** grain, crop in early Sumerian

 = **payir, nel** (பயிர், நெல்) 'crop, grain' in Indus Script

 = **šu** 'hand' in Sumerian

 = **kay** (கை) 'hand' in Indus Script'

 = **gal** 'big /great' in early Sumerian

 = **peru, pēr perum** (பெரு, பேர், பெரும்) *'big, great'* and

neṭu, nīḷ, neṭum (நெடு, நீள், நெடும்) *'long, tall'.* The sign is named as **peru** (பெரு).

 = kur 'mountain' in Sumerian

 = **kuṟinci** (குறிஞ்சி) *'hilly area'*; also, **toṭu; paṭu** (தொடு; படு), *'touch'* in Indus Script; phonetic syllable **kuṟa /kuṟi / kuṟu** (குற /குறி / குறு).

Observe that the sign consists of three triangles ***touching** each other* at one point, hence it is also associated with the concept of ***touching***.

The sign is named as **toṭu** (தொடு).

From the same inspiration, the Harappans devised another sign,

 = **varai** (வரை) 'mountain' in Indus Script.

5.05 Next, we are going to introduce a ***very important sign*** in the Indus Script. It is motivated by Egyptian Hieroglyphics.

X = **wpj** pronounced *wepej* in Egyptian to mean 'divide, distribute, share' and the Indus sign motivated by the above hieroglyph is:

X = logogram **pākam** (பாகம்); phonetic syllables **paku, paka, pā** (பகு, பக, பா). The sign is named as **paku** (பகு).

Champollion le Jeune is considered to be the doyen among the decipherers of Egyptian Hieroglyphic. His dictionary of Egyptian language is the most authoritative work in the field. The first-ever deciphered sign given by him is **'sky' (*ciel*** in French**)**; the Harappan Scholars adopted this sign. The sign denoting 'Ciel (sky)' in hieroglyphics is:

In the Indus Script, this sign is **not** used as a principal logogram, but used as an auxiliary sign in three shapes with the phonetic value **vān** (வான்) 'sky'.

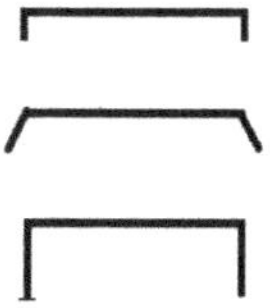

Here are some of them:

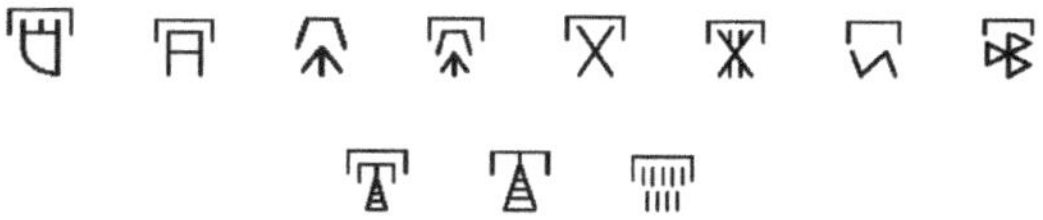

In many words, this auxiliary sign, in fact, a **diacritic,** adds to the qualified logogram the phonetic sound **vān** 'வான்', **pān / pāṇ** 'பான் / பாண்' as endings (**p** has voiced sound **'b'** in the middle of a word as the usual variant of '**v**'). However, there is a strong possibility that the sign  was used as primary sign for **vān** (வான்) *'sky'*. For example:

 = **toṭuvān** (தொடுவான்) 'horizon'

= **paṭuvān** (படுவான்) 'west / sunset'

 = **onpān** ஒன்பான் (*'nine, ninefold'* classical adjective form); *usually denoting the group of* ***nine planets of Indian Astrology*** *(nava-graha).*

5.06 However, we are going to learn another important word. There are two hieroglyphic signs which may be considered as the two halves of the sign X with minor modifications:  one means ***'walk forward'*** and the other ***'walk backward'***. If you rotate the second sign by 180^0 and place it over the first, we get:

Hence, the Indus sign X has been ascribed additional logogram value **kaṭa** (கட) *'cross'* and it is **very important** because it serves as the *base* of the word **kaṭavuḷ** (கடவுள்) 'God'.

We are going to study shortly in the ensuing sections that the double stroke sign || with logogram-value **iru** (இரு) *great'* serves as the **'divinity determinative'** equivalent to Mesopotamian **'an / dingir'.**

You can bear in mind that this **iru** (இரு) became the famous Dravidian term, **tiru** (திரு) in later period.

X + *(divinity sign)* || became the complex sign  to be interpreted as **kaṭavuḷ** (கடவுள்) *'God'*; similarly,

 = **pakavān** (பகவான்) 'God'.

However, I interpret  as **pakavu** (பகவு) 'share'; you can always make headway in the Indus Script Interpretation if you presume the *overhead roof-cap* as meaning the phonetic syllable **'u'** or **'vu'.**

 = **kaṭavul** (கடவுள்) *'God'.*

 = **pakavān** (பகவான்) *'Celestial God, Supreme Being'*

 = **pakavu** (பகவு) *'share'*

 = **mītu-poli** (மீது-பொலி) *"God's share of crop"*

5.07 On the other hand, the Indus Scholars took liberty to enlarge their stock of logograms, basing their ideas on shapes of things around them. For instance, they have introduced:

 = **kōḻi** (கோழி) 'fowl, hen, cock' in Indus Script.

 = **kōṭṭai** (கோட்டை) 'temple', 'palace', 'fort'.

 = **kōvaṇam** (கோவணம்) [Te. *gōvaṇamu*, Ka. Tu. *kōvaṇa*, Ma. *kōvaṇam*.] *man's under-garment loin cloth*; it is a pure Dravidian word, which has been borrowed by Indo Aryan Languages as *kaupīna. Please see the spellings in Telugu, Kannada and Malayalam.*

 = ēḻu (ஏழு) *'seven'*

 = **āṟu** (ஆறு) *'six'*

We are going to learn that as in the case of Egyptian Hieroglyphs and Mesopotamian cuneiform, it is not always possible in Harappan Language or Classical Tamil to prescribe the first syllable of a multi-syllabic word as the derived phonetic syllable, because out of 18 consonants only 9 can begin a word. ***When you need a phonetic syllable beginning with any of the other 9 prohibited consonants, the Harappan scholars used the second or last syllable for the purpose.***

Further, if you already have a sign for the first syllable of a word; then you can use only the second or last syllable for generation of phonetic syllables. Let us see how these two criteria works.

5.08 Consider the word, **kō + ḻi = kōḻi** (கோழி). There is already a sign for the first syllable, **kō =**  or  (கோ), the second syllable **ḻi** (ழி) begins with a prohibited consonant **ḻ** (ழ), hence you cannot find a word beginning with that consonant. Hence, the sign may serve a phonetic syllable for the second syllable, namely, **ḻi** (ழி).

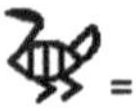 = **kōḻi** (கோழி) 'fowl, hen, cock' and phonetic syllable **ḻi** (ழி).

5.09 Consider the word, **kō + ṭṭai** = **kōṭṭai** (கோட்டை). There is already a sign for the first syllable, **kō** =  or  (கோ), the second syllable **ṭṭai** (ட்டை) begins with a prohibited consonant **ṭ** (ட்), hence you cannot find a word beginning with that consonant. Hence, the sign may serve a phonetic syllable for **ṭṭ** (-ட்ட-).

 = **kōṭṭai** (கோட்டை) 'temple', 'palace', 'fort' and phonetic syllable **-ṭṭ-** in mid-word position.

5.10 Consider the word, **kō + (v) + aṇam** = **kōvaṇam** (கோவணம்) where **v** is a euphonic add-on. There is already a sign for the first syllable, **kō** =  or  (கோ); hence, the second **nirai** syllable **aṇam** (அணம்) may serve as phonetic syllable as **aṇam** (அணம்) or **-ṇam** (-ணம்). Because of its rarity of use, the **nirai** syllable is also used for similarly placed phonetic value, **anam** (அனம்) or **-nam** (-னம்).

 = **kōvaṇam** (கோவணம்) [Te. *gōvaṇamu*, Ka. & Tu. *kōvaṇa*, Ma. *kōvaṇam*.] *man's under-garment loin cloth* and phonetic syllables, **aṇam** (அணம்) or **-ṇam** (-ணம்) and **anam** (அனம்) or **-nam** (-னம்).

The sign is motivated by Egyptian signs:

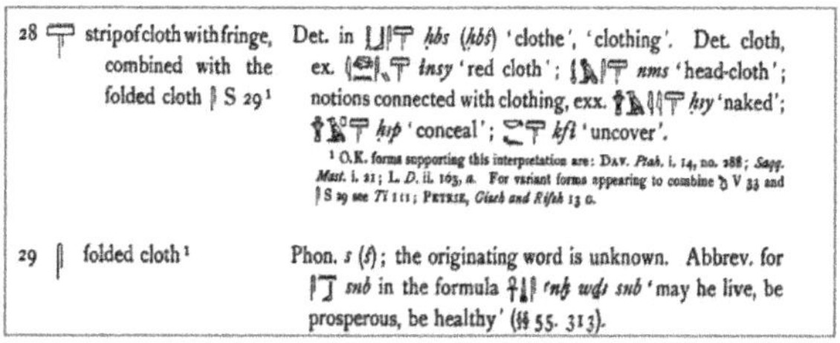
28 [sign] strip of cloth with fringe, combined with the folded cloth [sign] S 29[1] — Det. in [signs] *ḥbs* (*ḥbś*) 'clothe', 'clothing'. Det. cloth, ex. [signs] *insy* 'red cloth'; [signs] *nms* 'head-cloth'; notions connected with clothing, exx. [signs] *ḥsy* 'naked'; [signs] *ḥꜣp* 'conceal'; [signs] *kfi* 'uncover'.

[1] O.K. forms supporting this interpretation are: DAV. *Ptah.* i. 14, no. 288; *Saqq. Mast.* i. 21; L. *D.* ii. 103, *a*. For variant forms appearing to combine [sign] V 33 and [sign] S 29 see *Ti* 111; PETRIE, *Gizeh and Rifeh* 13 *a*.

29 [sign] folded cloth[1] — Phon. *s* (*ś*); the originating word is unknown. Abbrev. for [signs] *snb* in the formula [signs] *ꜥnḫ wḏꜣ snb* 'may he live, be prosperous, be healthy' (§§ 55. 313).

Cited for illustration purpose from Egyptian Grammar of Gardiner.

5.11 Consider the word, **ē + ḻu = ēḻu** (ஏழு). There is already a sign for the first part, **ē** = 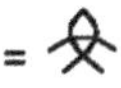 (ஏ), the second part **ḻu** (ழு) begins with a prohibited consonant **ḻ** (ழ்), hence you cannot find a word beginning with that consonant. Hence, the sign may serve a phonetic syllable for **ḻu** (ழு).

 = ēḻu (ஏழு) *'seven'* and the phonetic syllable **ḻu** (ழு).

5.12 Consider the word, **ā + ṟ = āṟu** (ஆறு). There is already a sign for the first part, **ā** =  (ஆ), the second part **ṟu** (று) begins with a prohibited consonant **ṟ** (ற்), hence you cannot find a word beginning with that consonant. Hence, the sign may serve a phonetic syllable for **ṟu** (று).

 = **āṟu** (ஆறு) *'six'* and the phonetic syllable **ṟu** (று).

We have introduced the following phonetic syllables which are not the first syllable or first portion any logogram.

(1)  = **kōḻi** (கோழி) 'fowl, hen, cock' and phonetic syllable **ḻi** (ழி).

(2)  = **kōṭṭai** (கோட்டை) 'temple', 'palace', 'fort' and phonetic syllable **-ṭṭ-** in mid-word position.

(3)  = **kōvaṇam** (கோவணம்) *man's under-garment loin cloth* and phonetic syllables, **aṇam** (அணம்) or **-ṇam** (-ணம்) and **anam** (அனம்) or **-nam** (-னம்).

(4)  = ēḻu (ஏழு) *'seven'* and the phonetic syllable **ḻu** (ழு).

(5)  = **āṟu** (ஆறு) *'six'* and the phonetic syllable **ṟu** (று).

Let us now proceed with some other interpreted signs.

 = **kākkay** (காக்கை) *'crow',* **kār, kāḷ , karu /kari** (கார், காள், கரு/கரி) 'black' in Indus Script.

 = **ulam** (உலம், உலக்கை) 'pestle' in Indus Script.

 = **kalam** (கலம்) 'vessel, cup, basket, mortar' in Indus Script.

 = **ulamkalam, ural** (உலங்கலம், உரல்) 'pestle and mortar' in Indus Script' Note that this is a complex sign combining two independent signs:

 **ulam** (உலம்) 'pestle' **+**  (கலம்) 'mortar' **=**  (உலங்கலம்) **/ ural** **(**உரல்) **/ cekku** (செக்கு) *'pestle and mortar / grinder / oil-press etc.'*

It is an important sign and plays a vital role in the Indus Script.

5.13 The next important sign introduced by the Indus Scholars relates to granary, particularly the one set up in the paddy field itself at the time of harvest; the traditional granary in ancient lands in general and the Harappan area, in particular, is ***of conical shape made up of twisted thick rope.*** The sign created by the Harappan scholars is:

 = **tombai (**தொம்பை) and also the logogram **'tumpai'** (தும்பை), name of a well-known shrub of South Asia; since the words involved are disyllabic, the first syllable is used as derived *phonetic syllable*, **to / tu** (தொ / து)

This sign was frequently used in Harappan writing, both as logogram and phonetic syllable. For example, a frequently occurring pair in the Indus Inscriptions is  which can be read as:

 = **tu** (து);  = **varai** (வரை)

 = **tuvarai** (துவரை), Harappan name for the city-state ***Dwaraka***. The word **tuvarai** (துவரை) occurs in Tamil Sangam Literature.

5.14 Another sign of importance devised by the Harappan scholars is a versatile sign used for the concepts like <u>*port / harbor, public pools with steps, chamber*</u>:

 = **tuṟai** (துறை) *'port, harbour'*

kaṭṭu (கட்டு) *'building'*

paṭi (படி), *'steps',*

aṟai (அறை) *'chamber, cell, room'*

An analysis of Indus Inscriptions reveals that this sign frequently occurs in double as . There is an important observation about double signs, which I should share with the readers as early as possible; it is almost like a rule governing the functioning of the Indus Script.

<u>Guideline 06</u> *Usually, a sign in the Indus Script has more than one logogram values and a couple of phonetic syllabic values; whenever such a sign occurs in double,* ***it is almost an unwritten law that each component of the double sign will have a <u>different</u> value****, never repetition of the same value. This result is applicable to triple or quadruple occurrence of a sign also.*

 = *tuṟai kaṭṭu, tuṟai paṭi, tuṟai aṟai,*
kaṭṭu tuṟai*, kaṭṭu paṭi, kaṭṭu aṟai,*
paṭi tuṟai, paṭi kaṭṭu*, paṭi aṟai,*
aṟai tuṟai, aṟai kaṭṭu, aṟai paṭi

There are in all 4 x 3 = 12 possible combinations; but all of them may **not** be meaningful ones used in practice. Only a few may pass over to actual usage, say for example, **kaṭṭu tuṟai** (கட்டுத் துறை)**, paṭi tuṟai**(படித் துறை)**, paṭi kaṭṭu** (படிக் கட்டு).

5.15 There is another important sign which often occurs in pair, even in the famous Large Sign Board of Dholavira, namely, the **sign** of

divinity, authority, government from time immemorial in this sub-continent, namely, the ***dharma chakra*** or <u>*dhamma chakka*</u>, அற (dharma) + ஆழி (chakra) = அறவாழி

 = **araicu** (அரைசு) or **aracu** (அரசு) *government'*, **āṭci** (ஆட்சி) 'rule'

When it occurs in pair it is interpreted as

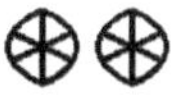 = **aracāṭci** (அரசாட்சி) 'government rule'

5.16 Another sign of importance created based on **taṟi** (தறி) 'wooden post', 'stake' meant for tying cattle is:

 = **taṟi** (தறி) *'stake'*; phonetic syllable dental **t** (த) and dental sibilant **s** **(ஸ)**, as adopted from Tamil Lexicon:

> தறி[3] taṟi , *n.* [K. M. *taṟi.*] 1. Cutting down, chopping off; 2. Wooden post, stake; 3. Pillar, column; 4. Peg; 5. Weaver's loom; etc...

You may wonder how come the dental **t** (த) and dental sibilant **s (ஸ)** can have the same sign. Bear in mind that the English words **think** and **then** are pronounced almost as **sink** and **zen in continental Europe,** particularly by **the French.**

You may also raise the question as how to reasonably assign two important sound values for a single sign. In this regard, we have ample evidential examples in Modern English and French.

In English, the letter **c** is pronounced both with **k** sound (*e.g.,* **cake, cater, criminal** etc.) and **s** sound (*e.g.,* **centre, race, cypher** etc.)

In French, the letter **c** is pronounced both with **k** sound (*e.g.,* **camion, côte, coin** etc.) and **s** sound (*e.g.,* **centre, grimace, cette** etc.)

Further, it is a well-known fact that **-nt-** after vowel sounds **i** and **ai** is pronounced as **-nc-** in Spoken Tamil and the the double consonant **-tt-** is pronounced as **-cc-** in Spoken Tamil. **In Malayalam,** they are, in fact, spelt as **-nc-** and **-cc-** in their written language also.

5.17 The examples so far cited in hieroglyphic, cuneiform or Indus Script, bear some reasonable resemblance to the objects depicted by them, but it is not always the case. The following bear distant resemblance:

= **GAR / ninda** 'bread / food' in Sumerian

= **ab** 'cow' in Sumerian

Further, it so happens that some basic signs bear no resemblance **at all** to the objects they depict. For example, the following sign seems to have absolutely no resemblance to the object it means, namely ***sheep,*** *udu*

5.18 On the other hand, several ideas which cannot be picturised are spelt in phonetic syllables as in Modern languages.

For example, in the Indus script, there are no specific logograms for <u>*food*</u> *or* <u>*cow*</u>*, instead they have been* ***spelt with phonetic syllables****, long a* **(ā)** *for cow and* **ūṇ** *for food. We'll be learning them shortly in subsequent chapters:*

 **= ā** (ஆ) 'cow'

 **= ūṇ** (ஊண்) *'food',*

Note carefully that there are **three** *small strokes inside the sign*  *which is the universal upper class ending, the* **an**-*sign.*

The **an**-sign with one small stroke inside denotes **in** (இன்)

 = **in** (இன்), **en** (என்);

The **an-**sign with two small strokes inside denotes **ān** (ஆன்)

 = **ān** (ஆன்); and

The **an**-sign with three strokes inside denotes **un / ūn / uṇ / ūṇ** (உன் / ஊன் / உண் / ஊண்).

 = **un / ūn / uṇ / ūṇ** (உன் / ஊன் / உண் / ஊண் and also ஒன் / ஓன் / ஒண் / ஓண் by replacing **u** by **o**.

We know that **ūṇ** (ஊண்) is the word for **'food'.**

5.19 In Harappan Language, nouns are divided into two broad categories known as ***tiṇai*** (திணை) *class'.*

<u>Gods and male humans</u> belong to ***uyartiṇai*** (உயர்திணை) *'upper-class'*; <u>female humans and others</u> belong to ***aĥṟiṇai*** (அஃறிணை) *non-class'.*

For the time being, bear in mind that,

 = **anṟu** (அன்று) is the universal **uyartiṇai** (உயர்திணை) *upper-class ending.*

In course of time, the **ṟu** portion has been omitted in <u>*South Dravidian I languages*</u> **(Tamil, Kannada and Malayalam)** but they have retained the **an** portion, while the <u>*South Dravidian II Language,*</u> **Telugu** omitted **n** and adopted **aṟu,** which later on became **aḍu.**

The name of the sign is **an** (அன்),

 = pronounced as **-i, -iy , -yi, -ai** (-இ, -இய், -யி, -ஐ) in the *case of **female humans*** and **-am -tu** (-அம், -து) in the *case of others,* is the universal **aĥṟiṇai** (அஃறிணை) ***non-class ending.***

The name of the sign is **iy** (இய்).

5.20 *Dear Reader, do you know one thing? You have **already** been equipped to **compose** a few meaningful words in the **Indus Script** which are already found in the excavated Indus inscriptions. **Only**, remember that the order of writing is from **right-to-left.***

Example A

 = **irai** (இறை) *'god, king'*

 = **an** (அன்) *Universal upper-class ending.*

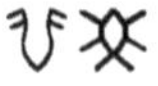 = **irai(v)an** (இறைவன்) **or irai(y)an** (இறையன்) *'god, king' with upper-class ending. The bracketed **v** or **y** is a euphonic consonantal **add-on**.*

 = **āḷ** (ஆள்) *'person'*, **aṭi** (அடி, அடிமை) *'slave, servant'*

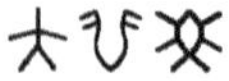 = **iraivan aṭi** (இறைவன் அடி) *'servant to god / king'*

There are more than 23 inscriptions containing  *in the Indus Valley from various sites of excavations. Here is a specimen from Lothal site meaning 'servant to God / King':*

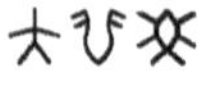 **8044 -2 -55**

***Guideline 04*** *In the inscriptions cited in this book, the given "four-digit number" is Mahadevan Index from his chef d'oeuvre, **The Indus Script: Texts, Concordance and Tables*** (Mahadevan, Indus Script : Texts, Concordance and Tables 1977). *The two-digit number refers to the site where the inscription in question was unearthed,*

11 for Mohenjo Daro,

22 for Harappa,

33 for Chandudaro

44 for Lothal

55 for Kalibangan

66 for Others

*The single digit 2, 3 etc. after Mahadevan index indicates that it is the second, third etc. **side** of the inscription.*

In the present example cited, it is the second side.

5.21 ***Example B***

In Sumerian Language the sign pair **'a-a'** is pronounced as **'ai-a'** (ஐ-அ - ஐய) and it means 'father'.

Coming to the Indus Script, we see that,

 = **ai** (ஐ) *'elder, leader, father'*

 = **an** (அன்) *Universal upper-class ending.*

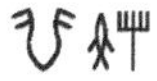 = **ai(y)an** (ஐயன்) *'elder, leader, father'* with upper-class ending. The bracketed **y** is euphonic *consonantal add-on*.

Let us now see the effect of adding the respect plural particle,  discussed above.

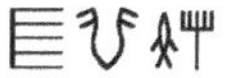 = **aiyanār** (ஐயனார்), *the famous village guardian deity.*

There are **thousands and thousands** of shrines, mostly open-air, dedicated to this village guardian deity in Tamil Nadu alone. Here is one specimen inscription in the Indus Valley,

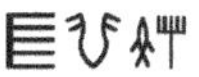 **1531 - 11**

Let us now add the 'good' adjective **nal (நல்).** There are a couple of temples with this name in Tamil Nadu. There is one famous temple at about 40 kms north of Tirunelveli as found from Google Maps:

 = **nal aiyanār** (நல் ஐயனார்)

Here are some specimen inscriptions from Mohenjo Daro and Harappa.

 **3249 -11**

 **4352 -22**

How about seeing our **nal aiyanār** in a Harappan Tablet in bas-relief? (***Cited purely for reference and research purpos)***

5.22 *A Very, Very Important Example C:*

You may be wondering as to why I have not given an example with the basic fish sign interpreted as logogram for **aṟa (அற)** *dharma* and as phonetic syllable, short vowel **a.**

 = **aṟam** (அறம்) *'dharma'*

 = **an (அன்)** *Universal upper-class ending.*

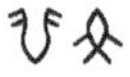 = **aṟavan** (அறவன்) *'God, sage, ascetic'*

Now look at the famous Indus Valley **Yogi** sealing:

Cited for research and reference purpose.

Observe the left top corner of the legend, it says:

 = **aṟavan**

5.23 ***Example D:***

We have seen that:

 = **ā** (ஆ) 'cow, cattle, property'

 = **uṭai** (உடை) 'possession, wealth, dress', **uṟai** (உறை) 'home, residence'

Can you read the following expression?

 = **ā + uṭai + an** = ஆ + உடை + அன் **>>** **āvuṭaiyan** (ஆவுடையன்) = a person possessing wealth, a *'Rich person'.*

There are inscriptions containing this text, such as the one found in Harappa:

 **4269 -22**

5.24 ***Example E:***

Now some examples with the Universal non-class **(ahriṇai)** ending  with *female specific* phonetic syllables **-i, -iy , -ai** (-இ, -இய், -ஐ).

iṟai + i >> iṟai +(v) + i >> iṟaivi (இறைவி) where v is a euphonic add-on.

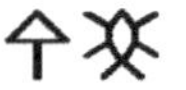 = **iṟaivi** (இறைவி), *'Queen, Goddess'* later on identified with Pārvati, Siva's female cohort during Vedic period'.

Here are two real time inscriptions from Mohenjo Daro

 **2161 - 11**

 **2280 - 11**

There are in all more than **29** such inscriptions found from various other sites.

5.25 ***Example F:***

ai + i >> ai +(y) + ai >> aiyai (ஐயை) where y is a euphonic add-on. When a syllable ending in **i** takes on the suffix **i,** the latter becomes **ai.**

 = **aiyai** (ஐயை), a female Goddess. Please see what Tamil Lexicon says:

ஐயை aiyai = Deities like Pārvatī; பார்வதி; Durgā; துர்க்கை. Kāḷī; காளி etc. and Mistress; தலைவி.

After Vedic Period, ஐயை aiyai came to be called Ishwari (*īśvarī*). We are going to learn an important Inscription later in this book.

We also have **aiyai** with the **'benevalence'** adjective or prefix **nal**

 = **nal aiyai** (நல் ஐயை). Please see the real time inscription from Mohenjo Daro.  **2183 -11**

Do you want to see how **aiyai** appears in Harappan tablet?

5.26 Here is a little digression. Simple expressions like '**he is**' and '**he has**' are respectively in French '**il est**' and '**il a**'.

In English '**he is**' becomes **'is he?'** in interrogation; and **'he has'** becomes **'has he?'** with reversal of order.

The rule for converting an affirmation into interrogation is the same in French, namely, *reversal of order.*

'Il est' becomes '**est-il?**', but **'il a'** does not become **'a-il?'** because the first word *ends in a vowel* and the second *begins with a vowel sound*; hence the expression takes on a euphonic consonant **t** as an **add-on** and becomes **'a-t-il?'**

Coming to Harappan Language, the compound fish sign  has the phonetic value **"ā"** and  is the universal upper class ending with phonetic value **'-an'.** The first sign ends in vowel sound and the second sign begins with a vowel, hence when they combine together, a sort of ***cacophony*** may occur and *there is need for some* ***euphonic add-on***. In this case it is the same **'t'** as in present day **French:**

 +  **= ā + an >> ā + t + an = ātan (ஆதன்),** 'sun god or father god'

 **= ātan (ஆதன்),** *'father god'*

Two simple instances in ***present day*** Malayalam and Telugu are appropriate in this regard:
(Malayalam) **ē** 'which' + **āḷ** 'person' becomes ē + t + āḷ = **ētāḷ** (ഏതാള്) '*which person*'.

(Telugu) **a** 'that' **+ aḍu** 'masculine ending' becomes a + t + aḍu = **ataḍu (అతడు)** *'that person'*.

In both the cases, the **euphonic add-on** is the same **'t'** as in French.

We have just now seen that **ā + an** becomes **ā + t + an = ātan.**
Please see real time inscriptions, the second one to be read as **ātan aṭi** *'servant or slave to ātan'*

 **3213 -11**

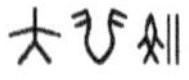 **4143 -22**

Same is the case with **ā + i** with *non-class* ending, some kind of euphonic add-on is required, it may not be only the usual **t.** We have others like **y**, double **t**, double **c** etc.

 = **āti, āyi, ātti, ācci** (ஆதி, ஆயி, ஆத்தி, ஆச்சி) all meaning **'mother or mother God'.** Please note the ***euphonic consonant clusters***.

Please see real time inscription from Mohenjo Daro given below:

 **1551 -11**

5.27 Further, the most frequently occurring feature in the etymology of any language is transformation of ***one consonant into another***; but there is no uniformity in world languages in this regard; each linguistic group follows its own rules, but the ones affecting the Harappan Language for the purpose of deciphering the Indus Script are those pertaining to Dravidian Languages.

These transformation rules can be identified from the exchanges amongst various Dravidian Languages. For example,

Tamil: **vatuvai** (வதுவை), *'marriage'*

Kannada: *maduve (ಮದುವೆ),*

Tulu: *madume.*

Note also ***ve, me*** endings in Kannada and Tulu.

Tamil: **vaṇṇān** (வண்ணான்)

Malayalam: **maṇṇān** (മണ്ണാന്)

I call it ***v-m exchange***. You can expect either **v** or **m** in Harappan Language.

5.28 Another important consonant exchange is **m-n** exchange. We have already met one in our discussions, nunai – munai, nuni – muni. The earliest one is in Tamil.

The archaic word, **nutal** (நுதல்) meaning forehead or *front* became **mutal** (முதல்) meaning 'front' or 'first'. The expression **'front row'** in English occurs as **'mutal varisai'** (முதல் வரிசை) in Tamil.

muppatu (thirty) is pronounced as **nuppatu** in some areas of Tamil Nadu. We have already discussed the possibility of lexical exchange between the NSI Language of Gangetic Valley and the ASI Language of Indus Valley and South India during Harappan period.

The Dravidian or Harappan expression **mu-kuṭṭu** (முக்கூட்டு / முக்குட்டு) *'tri-joint'*, the join of three roads, passed over to Indo Aryan languages as **nukkad** (नुक्कड़) *'tri-joint street corner'.*

We have already met the classical examples, **ammai – annai** *'mother';* and also செம்ம in Tamil and ಚೆನ್ನ in Kannada. *We can call this as **m-n exchange.***

5.28 Other consonant transformations which are relevant to the decipherment of the Indus Script and Language will be discussed as and when a necessity therefor arises.

Guideline 07 *Some of the **l**ong vowels found in closed form, (long vowel + consonant) in archaic words, have in course of time split into two cogent short vowels, transforming a **nēr** (நேர்) syllable into a **nirai** (நிரை) syllable.*

I have used here the descriptive word *'cogent'* to qualify the vowel, because sometimes **ō** splits into **u + a** instead of **o + a**, and **ē** splits into **i + a** instead of **e + a.**

Guideline 08 *Between the two split short vowels, invariably a euphonic consonant is added; usually it is **k** with voicing (that is '**g**' sound), **y** or **v** is the next choice.*

Here are some examples, which should be studied with care by the reader.

ām *(ஆம்)* **-->** *a + am* **-->** *a + k + am* **-->** **akam** *(அகம்) 'place, inside, house etc.'*

āl *(ஆல்)* **-->** *a + al* **-->** *a + k + al* **-->** **akal** *(அகல்) 'diva / oil-lamp'*

tūḷ *(தூள்)* **-->** *tu + a ḷ* **-->** *tu + k + a ḷ* **-->** ***tukaḷ*** *(துகள்)* *'dust / particle'*

mān *(மான்)* **-->** *ma + an* **-->** *ma + k + an* **-->** ***makan*** *(மகன்)* *'son, person'*

pāl *(பால்)* **-->** *pa + a l* **-->** *pa + k + a l* **-->** ***pakal*** *(பகல்)* *'daytime'*

nōr *(நோர்)* **-->** *nu + a r* **-->** *nu + k + a r* **-->** **nukar** *(நுகர்)* *'to smell'*

tēm *(தேம்)* **-->** *ti + a m* **-->** *ti + y + a m* **-->** ***tiyam*** *(தியம்)* *'sweet'; please bear in mind that* **tēn** *(தேன்)* *'honey' is a variant of* **tēm** *(தேம்).*

These Guidelines are important, because, as you are going to learn, one and the **same Indus sign**  serves to denote **pāl** *(பால்)* 'milk or white' as well as **pakal** *(பகல்)* 'daytime'

5.29 *On the other side, we also have:*

***<u>Guideline 09</u>*** *Some of the long vowels found in open form in archaic words, have in course of time split into a cogent short vowel plus* ***vu*** (வு) *transforming a* ***nirai*** *(நிரை) syllable into a* ***niraipu*** *(நிரைபு) syllable.*

Modern words:

nilā *(நிலா)* **-->** *ni + la + vu* **-->** **nilavu** *(நிலவு)* *'moon'*

kanā *(கனா)* **-->** *ka + na + vu* **-->** **kanavu** *(கனவு)* *'dream'*

irā *(இரா)* **-->** *i + ra + vu* **-->** **iravu** *(இரவு)* *'night'*

<u>**Archaic words:**</u>

kuṭā *(குடா)* **-->** *ku + ṭa + vu* **-->** **kuṭavu** *(குடவு)* *'bend, curve'*

palā *(பலா)* **-->** *pa + la + vu* **-->** **palavu** *(பலவு)* *'jack fruit'*

suṟā *(சுறா)* **-->** *su + ṟa + vu* **-->** **suṟavu** *(சுறவு)* *'shark'*

We have seen earlier that the vowel combo **ua = u + a** *is a variant spelling for long o* **(ō)** *and the vowel combo* **ia = i + a** *is a variant spelling for long e* **(ē).**

5.30 It sometimes happens that the combo, 'a **short vowel** + a **consonant** (usually liquid) + another **short vowel'** may occur as the combo, '**consonant** + a **cogent long vowel'.** For example:

ural (உரல்) >> ru + al >> r + ua + l >> **rōl (రోలు)**
ulakam (உலகம்) >> lu + akam >> l + ua + kam >> **lōkam (లోకము)**
avan (அவன்) >> va + an >> v + aa+ n >> **vān** **>> vāḍu (వాడు)**

6. *Signs for Abstract Concepts*

6.01 Are the concrete objects we meet in our day-to-day life, adequate enough to cover a spoken language?

What about the abstract concepts?

What to do with concrete objects that are ***not readily drawable***?

Such questions arise sooner or later. Particularly, it was felt that abstract concepts like *wealth, welfare, thinking, development, death, life* etc... adjectives like *rich, poor, quick, good, wrong, fast, slow etc...*, and grammatical terms like *in, to, from, at, etc...* could not be represented in the written form, but the ***Harappan Scholars paid their attention to this problem also and in fact they have successfully resolved them to certain extent.***

Following the set practice of Mesopotamians and Egyptians, the Harappans, too, have devised a couple of *signs exclusively for* ***"abstract concepts".*** Let us now examine two of such cases and leave others for future discussions.

The available signs were *quite inadequate* to serve the requirements of the spoken language. Further developments in the writing system were aimed at resolving these difficulties.

The scribes and scholars felt the need to extend the available stock of signs to take care of above situations by other means, namely, to extend the ***sense*** of an already existing sign denoting some concrete object to mean also some other cognate concrete or abstract concepts or similar looking objects.

ka 'mouth', rotated by 90° counter- clockwise at some stage in the development of Mesopotamian writing system as

 and caricatured in cuneiform as  was extended to concepts ***associated with or cognate with 'mouth'***, -`

(1) **zu** 'tooth',
(2) **kiri** 'nose',
(3) **eme** 'tongue', 'language'
(4) **dug** 'speak',
(5) **inim** 'word'.

Hence, the sign for 'mouth' was used to denote also any one of the above five concepts.

6.02 The Indus scholars readily adopted this compulsive extension in the writing system, in the Indus Script

 = **vāy** (வாய்) *'mouth'* was extended to logograms denoting

(1) **moḻi** (மொழி) *'say'*,
(2) **kūṟu** (கூறு) 'tell'
(3) **col** (சொல்) *'word'*,
(4) **vāyil** (வாயில்) 'entrance', *'gate'*.

Similarly, the logogram

 = **varai** (வரை) *'mountain'* in Indus Script was extended to logograms denoting

(1) **kal** (கல்) *'mount, rock, stone'*
(2) **kuṉṟu or kunṭu** (குன்று, குண்டு) *'hill, hillock'*
(3) **malai** (மலை) *'mountain'*, later form of **varai** (வரை)
(4) **mēru** (மேரு) *'huge mountain range like 'Himalaya' or 'Western Ghats'*

6.03 Another important extension used to assign additional meanings to the existing logograms, is to extend it to similarly **sounding** words with different meanings, namely**,** to ***homonyms***. This type of extension has earned a name for historical reasons, ***Rebus principle*** or ***extension by Rebus.*** We have already met several cases of Rebus Principle.

The following sign used to denote a *tumbler, cup, vessel* serves also ***'to drink'***:

 = **kalam** (கலம்) *'tumbler, cup, vessel'*

The ***first extension*** is to the verb associated with the noun, namely **kuṭi** (குடி) *'drink'.*

 = **kuṭi** (குடி) *'drink'*

However, the word **kuṭi** (குடி) *'drink'* has a homonym **kuṭi** (குடி) otherwise called **kulam** (குலம்) denoting ***'class or caste'.*** *By* ***Rebus principle*** *the sign is given* ***another extension*** *to mean social class or caste:*

 = **kuṭi,** (குடி) *'social class'*

Slowly, the purely logographic script developed into an admixture of logograms and phonograms; that is to say, the script began to evolve into a **logo-syllabic script**.

The Sumerians combined the signs for mouth and bread/food into a **complex-sign** to denote the concept, **eat:**

 **ka** *'mouth'* +  GAR, **ninda** *'bread/food'* =  **ka** *x* **GAR** = **gu** 'eat'

They combined the signs for 'man' and 'big' into a compound sign to mean the ruler or **king:**

 **lu** 'man' +  **gal** 'big /great' = 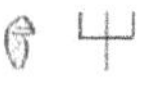 **lugal** 'king'

They combined the signs for 'woman' and 'dog' into a compound sign to mean **prostitute:**

 (**munus** *woman*) +  (**kur** *dog*) >>  (**nigu** *prostitute*)

There is a similar situation in the Indus Script: here the compound-sign should be read **right-to-left:**

 **peru,** (பெரு) *'big / great'* **+**  **mān / makan** (மான் / மகன்) **=** 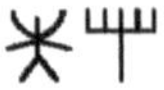 **perumān** (பெருமான்) *'king',* usually written with the compulsive upper-class ending **'an'** as

 **= perumān** *'king'* equivalent to Sumerian *'lugal'*

This text  occurs **34** times in Mahadevan's compilation of Indus inscriptions while the text without upper-class ending occurs **5** more times in the said compilation.

For example, the following are frequently occurring texts in Indus inscriptions:

U I = mutal kuṭi , (முதல் குடி) *'first social class (priests)'; we call it and pronounce the pair of signs as* ***antaṇar*** (அந்தணர்)

U II = irantām kuṭi, (இரண்டாம் குடி) *'second social class (soldiers, rulers)'; we call it and pronounce the pair of signs as* ***araiyar*** (அரையர்)

U III = mūṉṟām kuṭi, (மூன்றாம் குடி) *'third social class (merchants / traders)' ; we call it and pronounce the pair of signs as* ***vaṇikar*** (வணிகர்)

U IIII = nānkām kuṭi, (நான்காம் குடி) *'fourth social class (professionals / workers)'. Since vēḷ means 'profession' ; we call it and pronounce the pair of signs as* ***vēḷar*** (வேளர்).

Since there were only four social classes existing in the Indus Society, we have **not** come across **kuṭi** (குடி) sign with **5 or more** strokes.

Hence the four social classes are given below; the ***sign pairs should also be pronounced as such****:*

U I = ***antaṇar*** (அந்தணர்)

U II = ***araiyar*** (அரையர்)

U III = ***vaṇikar*** (வணிகர்)

U IIII = ***vēḷar*** (வேளர்)

Further, mention of class name seems to have been an important custom in Harappan society; whenever people submitted offerings to deities in temples, they invariably mentioned their **kuṭi** (குடி) *'class'* name on one side of their token-inscriptions, the other side being occupied by the deity's name or devotee's name.

Till recently, whenever devotees offer ***archana*** to **deities** in the temples, the priests used to ask for **gotra** (lineage) in addition to **name** and **nakshatra** (birth star); however, this practice seems *fortunately* to have been discontinued.

6.04 Complex and compound signs (a combination of 2 or more signs to generate a single sign with different meaning as in the above situations) are common both in Sumerian and Indus Script. Here are some more interesting cases.

This time a sign devised exclusively for **abstract concept** is given below.

The non-symmetrical sign  with *different left and right sides* is interpreted as **māṟu** (மாறு) *'differ /change'*. The symmetrical figure of the sign is shown in the second line of the picture below; it is symmetrical about the middle line drawn. Please also see how the part

A and Part B portions of the actual figure differ from each other. The picture is quite illustrative.

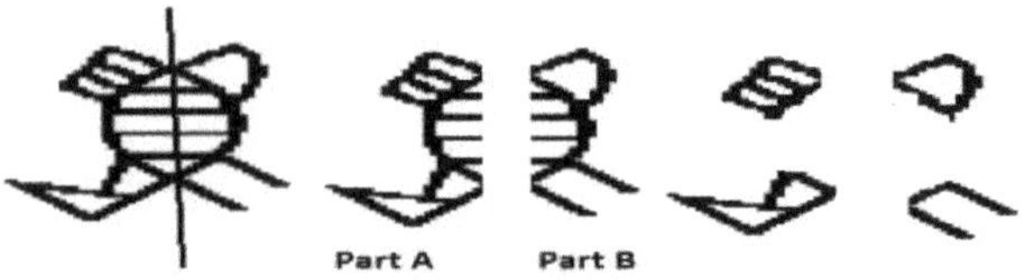

The symmetrical form

Earlier, we had a 'place' sign ; we highlighted the upper portion and produced a new sign  for 'upper /above'. Now we have devised an ***asymmetrical*** picture with ***differing sides.***

Iravatham Mahadevan has suggested that the sign  with asymmetrical sides may be considered as the one to convey the abstract meaning of **differ** / **change** by the word **'māṟu, māṟṟu'** (மாறு, மாற்று).

The word **māṟu** (மாறு) has a homonym meaning **sell**; by the application of **Rebus Principle**, the logogram is extended to this homonym also.

 = **māru** (மாறு) *'sell'*

Detailed explanation to this word is available in the Classical Kannada Dictionary compiled by Rev. Fr. Kettel.

Similarly, the sign  by virtue of its pictorial shape may be interpreted as **kolukki** (கொளுக்கி) *'hook'* with phonetic syllabic value **koḷ** (கொள்).

The word **koḷ** (கொள்) has a homonym meaning **buy**; by the application of **Rebus Principle**, the logogram is extended to this homonym also.

 = **koḷ** (கொள்) *'buy'*

For this term also, Detailed explanation is available in the Classical Kannada Dictionary compiled by Rev. Fr. Kettel. The reason as to why I give citation from Kannada source is that the above two terms are still used by Kannadigas with the same meanings. However, t*his is where* **Iravatham Mahadevan** *stopped and deviated elsewhere, but I tried to proceed to the* ***logical end.***

Let us continue the journey further in the newly discovered path.

 = **māṟu** (மாறு) *'sell'*

 = **koḷ** (கொள்) *'buy'*

Hence, when we can combine both of them to get:

 **māṟu-koḷ** (மாறு-கொள்) literally meaning ***sell-buy*** to be interpreted as **vaṇikam** (வணிகம் / விற்பனை) *'trade / business/ sale'*

Further the Indus sign  evidently meaning cross-roads is interpreted as **'kūṭṭu, kūṭam, kūṭal'** (கூட்டு, கூடல், கூடம்) meaning **'joint / crossroad / meeting-place'.** Now consider the chain,

 = **māṟu-koḷ-kūṭam** (மாறு-கொள்-கூடம்) literally meaning ***'sell-buy-joint'*** which can reasonably be interpreted as **ankāṭi** (அங்காடி) *'shop, market'*

If you add the upper class ending  **an (அன்)** equivalent to English *'-ist, -er, -man', the text* becomes:

 = **ankāṭian** (அங்காடியன்) *'shopman'.*

See the following inscription from Mohenjodaro:

 (Mahadevan No.2229)

6.05 I think that this is the right place to learn about another similarly placed sign of importance.

There are four signs in the shape of 'leaf' in the Indus Script:

 Out of these four only one could mean **'leaf'**. If so, what about the others? I am of the opinion that only the first sign denotes 'leaf'; it is also the simplest and plain picture; keeping these features of the sign in mind, the Harappans have included the abstract concept, **simple** also in the senses of the logogram:

 or  = **ilai / ela** (இலை /எல) 'leaf', **eḷiya / eḷimai** (எளிய / எளிமை), 'simple / simplicity'

From the shape, the second sign is interpreted as ***spear or lance***:

 or  = **vēl** (வேல்) 'dart, spear, lance'.

Since the dart, lance or spear was the most important and *primary weapon used by the Harappan people* for both peaceful hunting and defense / aggressive warfare, the sign was used for the generic concept of 'weapon'. A soldier carrying weapon was called **vēlan** (வேலன்) / **vēlappan** (வேலப்பன்) / **vēlayyan** (வேலய்யன்)

 = **vēlan** (வேலன்)

 = **vēlappan** (வேலப்பன்)

 = **vēlakkan** (வேலக்கன்)

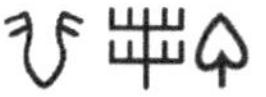 = **vēlayyan** (வேலய்யன்)

Guideline 09 *The suffixes*  **-appan** (-அப்பன்) *and* **-ayyan** (-அய்யன்) *are simply extended or fortified versions of the universal upper class ending* **-an**  *and they have nothing to do with the concept of '<u>father</u>'. To this duo we should also add* **-*akkan,*** *making it a useful* **trio**, *namely,* **-appan, -ayyan, akkan.**

This -akkan has later on become **-akkāran** (-அக்காரன்) as in **paṇakkāran** (பணக்காரன்) *'richman'*, **vēṭṭaikkāran** (வேட்டைக்காரன்) *'hunter'* etc.

6.06 Coming to the third sign , you cannot miss to observe the vertical line drawn as axis; the picture itself is symmetrical about this axis. In this picture, the axis is important; the meaning implied by the picture is the abstract concept of 'middle' **naṭu** (நடு) and its cognates 'straight', 'right'.

 = **naṭu** (நடு) *'mid'*, **naṭuvu** (நடுவு) *'middle'*, **nēr** (நேர்) *'straight'*, **cari** (சரி) *'right / correct'*

The frequently occurring pair  literally meaning '***middleman***' denotes a judge, while  **naṭuvu** (நடுவு) 'middle' indicates '***justice***'.

 = **naṭuvan** (நடுவன்) *'arbitrator'*, *'magistrate'*.

For referring to the **Judge of some superior court,** the determinative for **'divinity'** or **'authority',** which is *unpronounced*, is added, but the universal upper-class ending is pronounced with respect as **ar**:

 = **naṭuvar** (நடுவர்) *'Judge'*; please see for example the inscription found in Harappa,

 4268-22

The last or fourth picture requires more explanation. The middle line divides the figure into two parts. The additional set of strokes added on either side ***are not*** the same. Symmetrically speaking the picture is **'wrong', difficult'** as opposed to the meaning of ***right*** and ***simple*** ascribed to the plain sign. **That's it!** The sign implies the abstract concept of **'wrong'** and its **cognates.**

 = **tappu** (தப்பு) *'fault'*, **tavaṟu** (தவறு) *'wrong'*, **vaḻu** (வழு) *'error'*, **kuṟṟam** (குற்றம்), *'crime'* **piḻai** (பிழை) *'mistake'* *and also* **kaṭu** (கடு) *'difficult'*

At this point, we may note that the word **tappu** (தப்பு) 'fault' has an interesting *homonym* denoting **mēḷam** (மேளம்) *musical drum'*, a heritage drum instrument of South India. By application of **Rebus**, the sign denotes also this homonym.

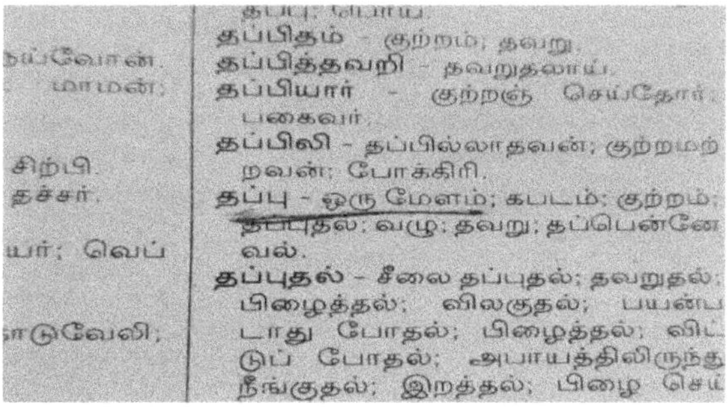
தப்பிதம் - குற்றம்; தவறு.
தப்பித்தவறி - தவறுதலாய்.
தப்பியார் - குற்றஞ் செய்தோர்; பகைவர்.
தப்பிலி - தப்பில்லாதவன்; குற்றமற்றவன்; போக்கிரி.
தப்பு - ஒரு மேளம்; கபடம்; குற்றம்; தப்புதல; வழு; தவறு; தப்பெண்ணேவல்.
தப்புதல் - சீலை தப்புதல்; தவறுதல்; பிழைத்தல்; விலகுதல்; பயன்படாது போதல்; பிழைத்தல்; விட்டுப் போதல்; அபாயத்திலிருந்து நீங்குதல்; இறத்தல்; பிழை செய்

Courtesy Kaḻaka Tamiḻ Akarāti (கழகத் தமிழ் அகராதி)

The musician who played this type of instrument was called **tappan** (தப்பன்) in Harappan Language.

 = **tappan** (தப்பன்) 'drummer'

There are several inscriptions containing this text. One sample each from Mohenjo Daro and Harappa are given below:

 **2908-11**

 **4016-22**

Try to compare the sign  with the similar one already learnt by us, namely,  **māru** (மாறு) 'differ / change'.

6.07 Here is an interesting example. Can you guess how to interpret the following *complex sign?*

A little digression for the ***methodology of reading complex and compound*** Indus inscriptions.

<u>Guideline 010</u> *Whenever two simple signs combine to form a single **complex** sign,*

(1) if <u>one of the component sign is bigger than the other</u> in size, then the convention of reading requires that the bigger sign should be read first followed by the smaller one;

(2) If both the components are of the <u>same size and occur side by side</u>, then the right-side sign should be read first and the left-side sign next;

(3) If both the components are of the <u>same size</u> and occur <u>one above the other</u>, then the upper sign should be read first and the lower sign next.

In the complex sign  both the components are of the same size, and one above the other, hence ***the upper one should be read first followed by the lower one..***

 = **naṭu** (நடு) 'mid', **naṭuvu** (நடுவு) 'middle', **ner** (நேர்) 'straight', **cari** (சரி) 'right / correct'

 = **(1) varai** (வரை) *'mountain'*

(2) **kal** (கல்) *'mount, rock, stone'*

(3) **kuṉṟu or kunṭu** (குன்று, குண்டு) *'hill, hillock'*

(4) **malai** (மலை) *'mountain'*, later form of **varai** (வரை)

(4) **mēru** (மேரு) *'huge mountain range like* 'Himalaya' or 'Western Ghats'

When we try to read by *using various combinations*, the best suited appears to be the one indicated below:

 **+**  **=** **naṭu (**நடு) + **kaḷ (**கல்)

 = **naṭukaḷ** (நடுகல்) *'Hero-stone'*

The largest number of artifacts unearthed during archeological excavations in South India in general and Tamil Nadu in particular, relate to small, monumental stones erected to the deceased war heroes of the past known as **naṭukal (**நடுகல்). Please see now the Indus inscription discovered at Kalibangan.

 8036-55

7. Indicate...Determine...

7.01 In this chapter, we are going to raise an important issue and try to resolve it also.

In any language, it may sometimes happen that several words mean the same thing; they are called **synonyms.** *Examples:*

large, big.
happen, occur.
splendid, fantastic.

On the other hand, there may be words with the *same phonetic values* but with different meanings. They are called **homonyms.**

Examples:

a. With same spellings:
tender (soft), **tender** (give);
saw (past tense of see), **saw** (a cutting tool);
right (side), **right** (correct).

b. With different spellings:
Hew (cut), **hue** (colour);
New (opposed to old), **knew** (past tense of know);
Hole (pit), **whole** (entire).

There are also words pronounced alike but differing in spelling and meaning, such as,

Rite, write, right, wright.

This is called **polysemy** as opposed to **polyphony**, words meaning same thing but with different phonetic values.

There may be occasions where a sign may mean several things and several signs may mean the same thing. *How to resolve such an issue?*

In this regard, the Egyptians, Mesopotamians and Harappans converged in unison and introduced two important elements in their writing systems:

(1) Determinatives,
(2) Phonetic Indicators.

These high-sounding technical jargons are likely to alarm the reader, but simple explanation through an illustrative example will definitely <u>*appease his mind*</u> and rekindle his interest in the subject.

The example involves ***pestle and mortar***. From the shape of the pictures, the following signs are reasonably interpreted as:

 = **ulam** (உலம்) *'pestle'*

 = **kalam** (கலம்) *'mortar'*

 **ulamkalam** (உலங்கலம்) *'pestle and mortar'*

Ulam (உலம்) became **ulakkai** (உலக்கை) in later periods and

ulamkalam (உலங்கலம்) became **ural** (உரல்)

 = **ural / cekku** (உரல் / செக்கு) *'pestle and mortar / oil-mill'*

Let us now examine some of the important verbs associated with **pestle-and-mortar** or **oil-mill**.

1. **arai** '**அரை**' (அரைத்தல்) 'to grind'.

2. **iṭi** '**இடி**' (இடித்தல்) 'to crush'.

3. **kuttu** '**குத்து**' (குத்துதல்) 'to pound'.

4. **āṭṭu** '**ஆட்டு**' (உரலில் மாவு ஆட்டுதல் 'grind flour in mortar', செக்கில் எண்ணெய் ஆட்டுதல்) 'mill oil in oil-press' 'grate'.

There are also other verbs like **poṭi** பொடி (பொடித்தல்), 'to powder or pulverize', **utai** '**உடை**' (உடைத்தல்) 'to break', but we are only going to concentrate on the above *four verbs* for the time being.

So, we have our sign  for pestle-and-mortar to denote **ulamkalam** (உலங்கலம்) or **ural** (உரல்), but what about the verbs associated with it.

Here comes the important concept of **determinative.** We already know that numeral strokes ***<u>are multi-functional</u>***, and we are going to study them elaborately in the chapters to follow.

7.02 Any casual scrutiny of Indus script inscriptions would reveal that the numeral stroke three ||| follows some logogram or the other instead of preceding it as is the case in Harappan or Dravidian Languages; an adjective precedes the noun it qualifies. I consider this three-stroke as **a determinative** to point out that the logogram it qualifies is used in **verbal sense.**

||| is one of the most frequently occurring pair in the Indus inscriptions; in fact, there are **124** instances where this pair occurs in the compilation of Iravatham Mahadevan. This combo determines verbs associated with pestle-and-mortar.

||| = **arai** (அரை), **iṭi** (இடி), **kuttu** (குத்து), **āṭṭu** (ஆட்டு) and **uṭai** (**உடை**)

The sign ||| used here is called a **determinative**. Determinatives play very important role in the Egyptian and Mesopotamian writing systems. *So is the case with Harappan writing also.*

Now arises the next logical question. The determinative ||| specifies that the qualified logogram  is used in the verbal sense. That is to say, the combo means any one of four verbs, **arai** (அரை), **iṭi** (இடி), **kuttu** (குத்து), **āṭṭu** (ஆட்டு); *but **'which one?'** is the next question.*

*Now makes gala entry, the next important concept of **phonetic indicator.***

Vowels and monosyllabic or multi syllabic words, which we already know, are used as Phonetic Indicators. In the present case, it is a field day for vowels. We know that:

 **= a** (அ),  **= i** (இ),  **= u** (உ),  **= ā** (ஆ)

 = **arai** (அரை)

 = **iṭi** (இடி)

 = **kuttu** (குத்து)

 = **āṭṭu** (ஆட்டு)

The ***phonetic indicators*** are meant for guidance only; hence they remain unpronounced.

At this juncture, an important aspect of Indus writing is relevant to be pointed out.

Guideline 011 *Whenever multi-valued signs or sign-combos are used, one of the values is considered principal and this value is utilised as* ***default value*** *of the sign or sign combo in the absence of any phonetic indicator. In fact, when the default value is intended,* ***then no phonetic indicator*** *is required.*

As means of guidance, we may consider two points to recognise the default value of a sign or sign-combo. If there are several values, the one beginning with the vowel sound ***'a'*** *is normally the default value. The second point is that the primitive value of a sign for which the sign was originally created is the default value of the sign.*

For example, the sign  *was created through motivation from the shape of crescent moon. It is a multi-valued sign with values,* ***al*** *(night-time),* ***irā*** *(night),* ***mati*** *(moonlight),* ***intu*** *(moon),* ***iruḷ*** *(darkness) etc. However, there are reasons to believe that the sign was originally created to cater to the generic Harappan word for moon,* ***intu.*** *Hence,* ***intu*** *is the principal value or default value of the sign. Phonetic syllabic value of the sign* ***nta*** (ந்த) *was derived from this sense only.*

Please bear in mind that reputed Indologists specializing in Sanskrit etymology, have opined that that the word **indu** is not of Indo-European origin, but only a **loan word** in Sanskrit.

In the present case, one of the values begins with the vowel sound **a**, therefore the default value of the sign combo  is **arai** (அரை) *'grind'.* So, if you want to use the sign combo in the sense of **arai**, it can be used without any phonetic indicator.

In Classical Tamil, **arai** meant also a **city state**. In ancient European civilization, we had city states like Athens in Greece, Rome in Italy etc. In antiquity also we had city states in Egypt (Memphis. Thebes, Alexandria etc.) and in Mesopotamia (Kish, Uruk, Ur, Nippur, Umma, Lagash etc.)

In fact, in the Indus Valley Bronze age civilisation, we had city states at Mohenjodaro, Harappa, Lothal, Dwaraka etc. Even after the decline of Indus Civilization, the migrating Harappans seem to have established city states in the South at Madurai, Pattinam, Korkai, Poompugar, Arukkamedu etc.

As we have the dichotomy of **nakar** and **nakaram,** we also have the dichotomy of **arai** and **araiyam.** We may concede that **arai** is the generic name for **metro,** while **araiyam** refers to some particular **city-state.**

Originally **araiyam was** written as  but in course of time the non-class ending has come to be used exclusively with female human nouns; as a result the ending was replaced by the phonetic syllable  **am (**அம்) and **araiyam** has come to be written as: 

7.03 In a previous chapter on vowels, we have learnt about the innovations of the Harappans, by way of **phonetic modifiers,**  (the vowel modifier) and  (the consonant modifier)

A **phonetic vowel modifier** transforms the first vowel sound in a logogram, <u>short into long or long into short</u>. Let us now examine how these concepts work in the Harappan Writing System.

The complex sign,

 = **ural** (உரல்)

When we add the *verbal-action determinative,*

 = **arai** (அரை), **āṭṭu** (ஆட்டு), **iṭi** (இடி), **kuttu** (குத்து)

Choosing one particular value,

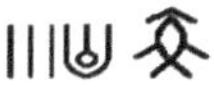 = **kuttu** (குத்து) *'grind'*

Let us now modify the first vowel sound (lengthen **u**) by adding the vowel modifier sign to get:

 = **kūttu (**கூத்து) *'dance, drama'*

With the above string, let us now add the universal upper class ending  **an:**

 = **kūttan** (கூத்தன்) *'actor, drama artist'*

Let us not stop here, but to proceed to add the *respect-plural particle* **ār** to get:

 = **kūttanār** (கூத்தனார்)

Kindly peruse the following **real-time Harappan Inscription**:

 4358 -22

Suppose we add the non-class ending instead of upper class ending, we get the word denoting ***female artist***.

 = **kūtti** (கூத்தி) *dancer, drama artiste'* (நடிகை, ஆட்டக்காரி)

Kindly peruse the following real time inscriptions from Mohenjo Daro:

 **1345 -11 -1**

 **2507 -11 -2**

Dancer - Google Safe Search - Labeled to reuse

 = **kūtti** (கூத்தி) *dancer*

7.04 We are now going to study another instance of *vowel modifier* and thereafter link it with the above example. We have already learnt the sign for palace, fort etc.

 = **kōṭṭai** (கோட்டை)

The first vowel sound in this logogram is a long vowel ō. Let us now shorten this vowel sound by adding the vowel modifier sign  to get:

 = **koṭṭai** (கொட்டை)

Adding to the string the phonetic syllable  **kai** (கை) we get:

 = **koṭṭakai** (கொட்டகை) *'theatre'*

In the Indus Inscriptions we have **kūttu (கூத்து)** *'dance, drama'* on one side and **koṭṭakai** (கொட்டகை) *'theatre'* on the other side. Then, is it not natural to expect their combination?

kūttu (கூத்து) *'dance, drama'* + **koṭṭakai** கொட்டகை) *'theatre'* = **kūttu koṭṭakai** (கூத்துக்கொட்டகை) *'drama theatre'*

The combination should be like the following string of signs:

In fact, there are inscriptions similar to the above, but the only difference is that the actual inscriptions *__lack the second modifier sign__* marked red (greyed).

From scrutiny of Indus Inscriptions, I have already formed the following unwritten law:

***__Guideline 012__*** *No modifier, indicator or determinative sign may occur more than once in a particular word or expression. The second such repeated sign is omitted, and the reader is expected to fill in the gap from his previous experience and knowledge.*

The real time expression is as follows with only one vowel modifier instead of the required two:

 = **kūttu koṭṭakai** கூத்துக்கொட்டகை

'drama theatre'

The string appears in the Indus Inscriptions as:

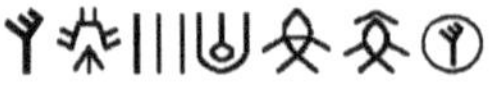 **1802 -11 -1**

 **3396 -11 -2**

The reader can now rest assured that there were **drama theatres** in the Indus Valley metros or city-states. We know how the ASI or Dravidian people now living in South India are fond of **cinema.**

Here is another example of vowel modifier from an entirely different arena. We have learnt earlier that:

 = **naṭuvan** (நடுவன்) *'judge, arbitrator'* where

 = **naṭu** (நடு)

Let us now add a vowel modifier to get,

 = **nāṭu** (நாடு) *'country'*

 = **nāṭan** (நாடன்) *'countryman, ruler, mountain-country leader, forest-country leader'*

With the above-mentioned meanings, the word appears in Sangam Literature ***hundreds of times***.

7.05 There seems to be a close connection between the Harappan civilization and the epic, Mahābhāratam.

Karṇa is one of the important leading characters of the Epic. He is elder to pāṇḍavas, the heroes of the story, but close associate of Kauravas, the villains of the story. He was king of **Anga** country, *which was probably in the Indus Civilization Area* near Dwaraka or **tuvarai,** the abode of **Krishna.**

We know that the complex sign  which is a combination of ( + ) **'am + kay'** has the sound value 'anga'. Hence, peruse the following inscription which occurs a couple of times,

 = **anka nātan** (அங்க நாடன்), *'ruler / inhabitant of Anga country'.*

A few inscriptions from Mohenjodaro:

 **3312 -2 -11 -1**

 **3343 -2 -11 -2**

 **3395 -11 -3**

 **3405 -11 -4**

7.06 We have seen ***how** the vowel modifier*  functions in the Harappan writing system. Now let us proceed to study ***how the consonant modifier***  functions by adopting the same methodology.

The complex sign,

 = **ural** (உரல்)

When we add the *verbal-action determinative,*

 = **arai** (அரை), **āṭṭu** (ஆட்டு), **iṭi** (இடி), **kuttu** (குத்து)

Choosing one particular value,

 = **kuttu** (குத்து) *'grind'*

Let us now modify the phonetic value of the expression by adding the consonant modifier. The added consonant modifier  modifies the double consonant **tt** into **nt**. The result will be that **kuttu** will become **kuntu**

 = **kuntu (குந்து)** literally meaning *'sit, take seat'*

Let us now add further the Universal *feminine specific* non-class ending  to get:

 = **kunti** (குந்தி)

The story of the Great Indian Epic, Mahābhāratam revolves around three prominent woman characters, namely**, Satyavati, Kunti** and **Draupati. Kunti was mother of Karṇa and Pāndavas,** who are the heroes of the Epic.

In the above example, the Harappan scribes felt that the rarely used consonant modifier alone is enough to identify the intended word and they omitted the vowel modifier considered redundant. There are not less than 3 inscriptions containing **kunti:**

 **1170 -11 -1**

 **2208 -11 -2**

 **5062 -22 -3**

Here is another example to learn the use of consonant modifier.
We know that:

 = **ā** (ஆ)

 = **ṭṭ** (ட்ட)

By application of consonant modifier,

 = **ṇṭ** (ண்ட)

 = **an (அன்)**

 = (ஆண்டவன்) *'god'*

This expression occurs in a Kalibangan inscription: code 55 refers to Indus site Kalibangan.

 **8062 -55 -1**

7.07 The ideas introduced and explained above are so important that the reader should have a very clear conception about them. It is not always the case that an additional vowel sign is inserted to indicate the correct phonetic value.

For example, the well-known sign  has basically three phonetic logogram values: **mē, mēl, mēṭu** (மே, மேல், மேடு). The **kūṭu** sign  serves among others as phonetic syllable **ṭu** (டு). Suppose we want to refer to the ***citadel*** called in Harappan **mēṭu** (மேடு), then what we do is to add a phonetic indicator after the primary sign to emphasise the fact that the second half has phonetic value **ṭu** (டு) as indicated below:

= **mēṭu** (மேடு), *'citadel'. Throughout this book,* the sign combo *will always denote citadel,* **mēṭu** (மேடு). In this example, the **kūṭu** sign is neither used as logogram nor as phonetic syllable, but it serves here as ***phonetic indicator, and it is not pronounced.***

However, it is quite interesting to note that the **mēṭu** *sign itself serves as phonetic indicator in some other connection for the same above phonetic value, namely,* **ṭu.** We'll now examine that example.

= **kōṭu** (கோடு), **kompu** (கொம்பு) *'horn'*

Both the ***synonyms*** are important words, but how to choose the desired one? We must have recourse to some phonetic indicator.

From the shape, the following sign is interpreted as:

= **pū** (பூ) *'flower';* as usual the sign also serves as indicator for the phonetic value.

Let us consider the two sign combos: &

In the first case, the **mēṭu** sign serves as phonetic indicator to the effect that the principal sign in question ends with the sound value **ṭu** (டு), hence,

= **kōṭu** (கோடு).

In the second case, the **pū** sign  serves as phonetic indicator to the effect that the principal sign in question  ends with the sound value **pu / pū** (பு / பூ), hence,

 = **kompu** (கொம்பு).

The personified versions in both the cases:

 = **kōṭan** (கோடன் / கோடங்கி) *'diviner, sooth-sayer'.* Real time example from Harappa is:

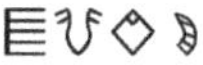 **4455 -22**

 = **kompan** (கொம்பன்) *'Tusked or horned animal / Clever man / Chieftan'.* Real time example from Harappa is:

 **4454 -2 -22**

7.08 The Indus Sign,  has some important interpretations such as, **varai** (*mountain*), **kunṟu** (*hill, hillock*), **kal** *(rock, stone)*, **malai** *(mount)*, **mēru** *(mountain range like Himalayas).* In my opinion the word **malai** is only a derivative of the archaic form **varai.**

The **naṇṭu** (நண்டு) sign,  has logogram value, **naṇṭu, nanṟu** (நண்டு, நன்று) etc. and phonetic value, **-ṇṭ-, -nṟ-** (-ண்ட்-, ன்ற்-). It is also used sometimes as phonetic indicator to the effect that the qualified sign has the phonetic value **-ṇṭu, -nṟu** (-ண்டு-, ன்று-). in the ending.

Hence, if you want to cull out the word, **kunṟu** (*hill, hillock*), for the sign,  then you can use this **naṇṭu** sign,  as phonetic indicator.

 = **kunṟu** (குன்று) as in Tamil or **kunḍu** (కుండు) as in Telugu. A repeatedly occurring text in Harappan inscriptions is:

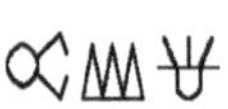 = **kīḻkunṟu** (கீழ்க்குன்று) *'Eastern Hill'*

where the **naṇṭu** sign  serves as ***phonetic indicator*** in order to choose the value of  = *(logogram)* **kal / varai / kunṟu / malai / mēru** as one ending with **- ṟu.**

kīḻkunṟu (கீழ்க்குன்று) *'Eastern Hill'* denotes, in my opinion, some place near Harappa city.

8. *Indicators and Determinatives: Some Examples*

8.01 At the outset, I would like to say a few words on the pronunciation of two important signs, namely,  and 

 *logogram* **payir, nel, pai** and *phonetic syllables* **pai, vai**

 *logogram* **pal, val, pai** and *phonetic syllables* **ār, gaḷ, kaḷ**

An important point that should be borne in mind in this connection is that Harappan language (Tamil also in the matter) does not make a difference between **voiced surds** and **unvoiced surds** in vocabulary building as in the case of most of other languages like English, French, Sanskrit, Hindi etc.

The letters, **k, t, p** etc. are *unvoiced (hard)* consonants.

The letters, **g, d, b** etc. are their corresponding *voiced (soft)* consonants.

However, voiced and unvoiced sounds ***do exist*** in Harappan and Tamil, regulated by conventional rules.

Generally speaking, a surd at the initial position of a word **or** when occurring as double-consonant **or** when following another surd is unvoiced (hard) and otherwise voiced (soft), that is, in the medial position of a word when flanked by vowels on either side or following a nasal consonant it is soft or voiced.

k in **k**aṭal (கடல்), pa**kk**am (பக்கம்) etc., **p** in **p**āl (பால்), a**pp**a (அப்பா) etc. are unvoiced (hard).

k in pa**k**al (பகல்), taṅ**k**am (தங்கம்) etc., **p** in **tu**ṇipu (துணிபு), am**pu** (அம்பு) are voiced (soft).

Further, the voiced surd **p** as in **tu**ṇipu (துணிபு) sometimes sounds as **v** as in **tu**ṇivu (துணிவு); this situation existed in Harappan period also.

The sign  with logographic phonetic value **pal** (பல்), while occurring in word-medial positions, sounds sometimes as **val**(வல்) which means 'strength' and in fact it is a derivative from **pal** 'tooth.'

An important example is examined below. The sign,  has logogram value, **kāval** and frequently used phonetic value, **kā**. However, there are two spellings for **kāvalan,** *viz.,*  **and** , the first is usually used to denote a security guard or watchman, ***a low rank official*** and the second refers to ***high rank officer*** and also the **King** himself; hence the difference with due deference to the King and other high officer; the sign is used with phonetic value, **val** as mentioned above:

 **= kā**

 **= val**

 **= an**

 **= kāvalan** (காவலன்)

Real time inscriptions ***with*** **:**

 **1118 -11 -1**

 **1343 -11 -2**

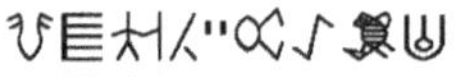 **2107 -11 -3**

 **2121 -11 -4**

 **2283 -11 -5**

 **4137 -22 -6**

 **4145 -22 -7**

 **4361 -22 -8**

Real time inscriptions ***without*** **:**

 **1078 -11 -1**
 **2403 -11 -2**
 **2557 -11 -3**
 **2935 -11 -4**
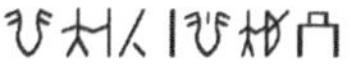 **3085 -11 -5**

Compare for example the 6th item in the first list and 3rd item in the second list.

8.02 Coming to the **payir** sign , we have a similar situation. The sign has the phonetic syllabic value **pai** as well as **vai**.

Here is an interesting, rare example. There is an inscription in Mohenjo Daro consisting of a solo sign on one side:

The sign is evidently a combination of the **todu** sign and **payir** sign as indicated below:

 =  **toṭu, paṭu** +  **payir, pai, vai**

I interpret it as, **paṭuvai (படுவை)**, meaning *'float'* otherwise called **teppam (தெப்பம்).**

 = **paṭuvai (படுவை)** *'float'*

The real time inscription is:

 **2264 -2 -11**

8.03 Incidentally, the **payir** sign  sometimes serves as phonetic indicator also. In the following text found in Mohenjo Daro, it is definitely a **phonetic indicator** advising the reader that the sign preceding it ends with the phonetic value **pai.**

 = **tompai (தொம்பை)**, not anything else. The whole inscription is:

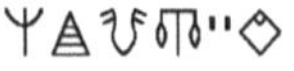 **1537 -11**

8.04 Phonetic Indicators are sometimes used to specify pronunciation of words with indeterminate endings. For example, the complex sign, has *indeterminate endings*, such as **a, e, æ, i, ai** etc. with phonetic values, **aṅka, aṅke, aṅkæ, aṅki, aṅkai** etc. When **aṅkai** is needed, they added the **ai** diphthong after the complex sign as phonetic indicator:

 denotes **ankai** (in classical Tamil period onwards **nankai** நங்கை or **mankai** மங்கை**)** ***lady***. Please see the following real time inscription in this regard; in fact, there are several similar to this one.

 **5230 -22**

8.05 In earlier chapters, we examined and discussed that some of the numeral stroke signs are used as determinatives. For example, the two stroke **iru** sign || For example, the two-stroke **iru** sign || when placed after a logogram serves as **divinity** determinative as in **amman** or **munian** (Mother Goddess or Deity Muni).

The numeral three-stroke **mutu** sign ||| when placed after a logogram serves as **verbal action** determinative as in the case of **arai** (grind or city state).

The numeral five-stroke **yā** sign ||||| when placed after a logogram serves as **motion** determinative as in the case of **vaṇṭi** (cart or chariot).

In a similar vein, the numeral seven-stroke **e̱lu** sign when placed **BEFORE** a logogram serves as **locative / building** determinative as in the case of **kōṭṭai** or **vīṭu** (fort or home).

At this juncture, it is interesting to note that in Mesopotamian cuneiform, most of the determinatives are usually placed **after** the qualified logograms; but the locative determinative **ki** is placed **after** the qualified logogram.

9. Strokes in the Indus Script

9.01 Strokes occur in the Indus Script in several sizes with different orientation and location. Unless we form a coherent theory about these strokes, it is impossible to make any headway in the interpretation of Indus signs.

Following the practice prevailing in Egypt and Mesopotamia, the Indus Scholars adopted strokes from one to nine as numerals to denote their number:

However, even a cursory analysis of these stroke signs in the **Harappan inscriptions** reveals that they are not used exclusively for counting purposes and *they are assigned functions other than simple numerals.*

From this chapter onwards, we are going to study the important strokes in depth one by one, first taking the single stroke | for analysis.

Appellation is always the first step; that is, the **roll call** is important. The primary logographic value of the one-sign is **oru** (ஒரு)

| = **oru** (ஒரு) *'one'*

Hence, let us *name* the one-stroke sign as **oru** sign.

In English, the indefinite article '**a**' has a variant '**an**' to be used before words beginning with vowels. In an exactly similar manner, **oru** (ஒரு) has a variant **ōr** (ஓர்) to be used before words beginning with vowels. Compare the usages:

oru nāḷ (ஒரு நாள்) *'one day'* **ōr iravu** (ஓர் இரவு) *'one night'*

So, the logographic value of the sign is naturally extended to the variant **ōr** (ஓர்).

The shape of the **oru** sign unmistakably suggests ***'pole', 'mast'*** or similar objects. Consequently, the value of the sign is extended to:

| = **kōl** (கோல்), **kaḻi** (கழி), **kampam** (கம்பம்), *'pole, mast, stick, rod, sceptre'*

The word **kōl** (கோல்) has an important homonym meaning 'weighing scales' otherwise called **tarāsu** (தராசு); by Rebus Principle the value of the sign is extended to 'weighing scales. Let us now combine the iconic values of the signs  and | to get:

| = **kōl** (கோல்) *'scales'*;

 = **mīn** (மீன்) *'star, planet, zodiac sign'*

 = **kōl mīn** (கோல்மீன்) *'zodiac sign **libra**' துலாம் இராசி'*

N.B. *It has been observed from the Indus inscriptions that whenever the fish sign is used in the **sense of a planet or a zodiacal sign**, the non-class (aḥṟiṇai) ending* ***-am*** *is added to give phonetic value* **mīnam** rather than **mīn.**

*The Zodiac sign Pisces was represented by double fish sign and probably pronounced as **mīn mīnam**:*

 = **mīn mīnam (மீன் மீனம்)** *"zodiac sign **pisces**"*

The real time inscriptions are found only with this non-class ending.

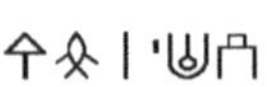 **2440 -11**

 **4232 -22**

The Zodiac sign Taurus is ***viṭai mīn*** *or* ***iṭai mīn*** *and represented by*

 = iṭai **mīnam** (இடை மீனம்) *"zodiac sign **taurus**"*

The real time sample is:

 1088 -11

9.02 The other phonetic-syllabic values assigned to the **oru** sign are:

r (ர்), **ru** (ரு), **r** (ர).

It may be borne in mind that the letter 'ra' used later in Tamil Brahmi or tamil̲i is a 'single stroke'; hence in all fairness, we may consider the Brahmi letter '**ra**' as an extension of the Indus Sign.

Later, the single stroke used by Tamil Brahmi has degenerated into double stroke with a join on upper side. This reformed sign is used both as consonant **ra** and as **long-vowel sign**. When used as long-vowel sign, it is called **leg** (கால்):

pānai பானை, **cāvi** சாவி, **tāli** தாலி

Compare at this point of discussion the compound sign **kā** in Devanāgari and Tamil Scripts:

का கா

In earlier days, Tamil used **-ா** sign for both **ra and** leg (கால்); in order to differentiate them, a small oblique diacritic is added to **ra** (ர). Even today, when we print **ri** (-ரி) or **rī** (-ரீ) we use **leg** (கால்) **-ா** for **ra** instead of (ர).

There is a reason as to why I have been so elaborately dealing with the issue. As in the present-days, even in the Indus Script, the single stroke was used as a diacritic sign for long-vowel particularly in complex signs as indicated below:

 = **ka** (க).

 = **kā** (கா).

 = **tu (து) / to (தொ)**

 = **tū (தூ) / tō (தோ)**

 = **ku(கு) / ko(கொ)**

 **or**  = **kū (கூ) / kō (கோ)**

 = **ppa** (ப்ப)

 = **ppā (ப்பா)**

In both Egyptian hieroglyphic and Mesopotamian cuneiform, the single stroke I serves **also** as a naming determinative. Roughly speaking, when this one-stroke sign is placed before a logogram, it indicates that the logogram has, among its various logographic and phonetic-syllabic values, its **name** as phonetic value; that is why it called a *naming determinative.*

**Guideline 013** *The one-stroke in the Indus Script performs* **also** *the function of* a *naming determinative as in* Egyptian hieroglyphic and Mesopotamian cuneiform, *but with a subtle difference. When the one-stroke is placed as the initial element of a text or word, it indicates that the text or word in question, is the name of an individual person.*

9.03 Anticipating what is in store in the later chapters of this book, let us say that  is a complex sign, arisen from two different sources. Details can wait for the time being. The complex sign has two sound values:

 = (1) **-amma-** (-அம்ம-) ,

(2) **-muruku (**-முருகு-)

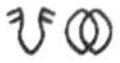 = **amman** (அம்மன்) ***'Mother God'***

murukan (முருகன்) ***'Lord Muruga'.***

Since the complex sign has multiple values, we need some kind of phonetic or semantic indicator to choose any particular word. In the present case, the word **amman** (அம்மன்) begins with vowel **'a'** it does not require any separate sign as phonetic indicator; for choosing the word **muru-an** or with euphonic consonant **k, murukan,** they add a phonetic indicator  (one of the three-stroke signs with phonetic value **mu**)

 = **murukan** (முருகன்);

Suppose the inscription refers to a person bearing the name of **murukan,** we require to add the naming determinative, one-stroke:

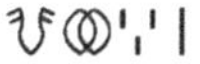 = **murukan** (முருகன்) *"a person's name"*

Please see an inscription from Mohenjo Daro:

 **3039 -11 -43**

9.04 we have just now learnt the *three* different uses of the one-stroke. How about an example illustrating all these three uses?

In ancient Tamil, **koṭu** (கொடு) means hill-top, mountain-top, summit etc. The sign chosen by the Indus Scholars is quite illustrative.

 = logogram **koṭu** (கொடு) and derived phonetic syllables **ku** (ku) **/ ko** (கொ)

From the shape of the sign, they have extended its applicability to **kuvi** (குவி) *'converge' and* **mūṭu** (மூடு) *'close'*

 = **kodu** (கொடு) *'crest', 'summit',* **kuvi** (குவி) *'converge';* phonetic syllables **ku** (கு), **ko** (கொ) **vu** (வு) **vo** (வொ).

We may name the sign as **kodu** (கொடு).

When you rotate this sign 180°, we get its vertical flip which has been assigned the following related but opposite meanings:

V = logograms **vānku** (வாங்கு) *'receive'*; **viri (விரி)** *'diverge, spread'*; and phonetic syllables **vi** (வி) / **ve** (வெ)

We may name the sign as **vānku** (வாங்கு).

It may, however, be noted that both these signs use the *one-stroke* sign for lengthening of vowel sound:

ko, ku (கொ, கு) + *leg*(கால்) = **kō, kū** (கோ, கூ)

Λ + | = ↑ **or** ⌃ **kō, kū** (கோ, கூ)

kō means **'king'**

V + | = Ѱ **vī / vē** (வீ / வே)

vī means **'bird'**

The sign Ѱ should not be confused with Ш; both are different, however this sign has fallen into disuse and replaced by Ш in order to avoid visual confusion as in the case of merger of overlapping circles and overlapping ovals.

9.05 Let us now examine an interesting example where the one-stroke is used as phonetic syllable **ra.**

Take the text |Λ for scrutiny; we already know both the individual signs.

Λ = **koṭu** (கொடு) *'summit'*, **kuvi** (குவி) *'converge'* and phonetic syllables **ku** (கு), **ko** (கொ)

| **=** phonetic syllables **r (ர்) , ra** (ர), **ru** (ரு)

Combining both we <u>can</u> get:

koṭur கொடுர், **koṭura** கொடுர, **koṭuru** கொடுரு,

kuvir குவிர், **kuvira** குவிர, **kuviru** குவிரு,

kor கொர், **kora** கொர, **koru** கொரு,

kur குர், **kura** குர, **kuru** குரு,

Out of these only the following three are found to be meaningful: **kuvir** குவிர், **kuvira** குவிர, **kuru** குரு.

kuvir குவிர் / **kuvira** குவிர relate to the guardian-deity of **kūla vaṇikam** (கூல வணிகம்) *Groceries business.* Later in Sanskrit based literature, this deity had come to be called **Kubera,** god of wealth.

Kuru is the founder of **kuru dynasty** in the Classic Epic, Mahābhāratam. There are indications that this epic was closely associated with the Indus Civilization and people.

|Λ = **kuvira** (குவிர) relate to the guardian-deity of **kūla vaṇikam** (கூல வணிகம்)

It is also relevant to point out at this juncture that the deity-name, **kuvira** (குவிர) continued for long with the Dravidian Diaspora. For, this deity name **kuvira** (குவிர) and the father-god name already met, **ātan** (ஆதன்) are found together in an artifact unearthed ***<u>recently</u>*** in the **vaikai-porunai** (வைகை-பொருநை) excavations near **kīḻaṭi** (கீழடி).

The writing is in Tamil Brahmi or **tamiḻi** script.

Ātan in Indus script 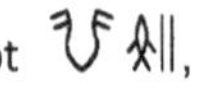, in **tamili** 

kuviran in Indus script 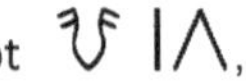, in **tamili** 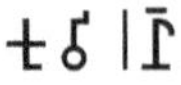

Observe the red-coloured (greyed) one-stroke in both Indus and **tamili** Scripts, with the same phonetic value **ra**

This artifact was radiocarbon dated by US based Beta Analytic Testing Laboratory and found to be 2700 years old, <u>400 years prior to the earliest Ashoka Edicts in Brahmi script</u>. Hence, there is a fat chance that the scholars in the court of North Indian king, Ashoka could have very well adopted the **tamiḻi** script already in vogue in the South, for creation of his Brahmi script.

tamiḻi could have been introduced to Ashoka by the roaming Buddhist and Jain monks, who frequently visited the South India and Sri Lanka for propagation of their religious doctrines.

9.06 Next, let us examine the following inscription found in Harappa:

 5102 -22

We already know how to interpret each of the signs in the above text.

The sign ⛨ has logographic value **tompai / tumbai** (தொம்பை / தும்பை) and phonetic syllabic values **to** (தொ) / **tu** (து). However, the naming determinative placed before the logogram indicates that only logographic value should be taken into account.

Hence, ⛨ has phonetic value **tompai / tumbai** (தொம்பை / தும்பை). **Tompai** is granary and **tumpai** is the name of a white colour shrub flower.

As we have discussed somewhere earlier, the combo 🏳◇ has an interpretation, mēṭu (மேடு) *'citadel, mound'*

🏳◇⛨| = **tompai mēṭu / tumpai mēṭu** (தொம்பை மேடு / தும்பை மேடு). Most probably, it could have been the name of a place. An interesting fact is that even today there is a place named **tumpai mēṭu** (தும்பை மேடு) in Tamil Nadu as found from Google Maps.

Tumpai with botanical name, *Leucas aspera,* is an important plant in the whole of South Asia fully covering the erstwhile Harappan Civilization area. Hence the probability is very high that the expression could have denoted an ancient place name in Indus Valley.

Thumbai shrub in a Chennai suburb

10. Double stroke

10.01 One of the most versatile signs in the Indus Script is unmistakably the frequently occurring double stroke || This sign has several functions, and it is quite profitable to examine them all in detail at one place.

Iconic phonetic values of the sign requiring no further explanations are:

|| = **iranṭu** (இரண்டு) / **iru** (இரு) with its variant before vowels **īr** (ஈர்) *'two'*; and **īr** (ஈர்) / **īram** (ஈரம்) *'water'*.

Phonetic syllabic values are:

|| = **iru** (இரு) **and** **iri** (இரி).with its variant before vowels **īr** (ஈர்).

I am of the opinion that the phonetic value **i (இ)** should also be included for etymological reasons. For example, Tamil / Malayalam **irupatu/iruvatu** (இருபது/இருவது) *'twenty'* occurs in **Kannada** as **'ಇಪ್ಪದು'** (ippatu இப்பது) after elision of **r** sound.

I name the logogram || as **iru.**

On the other hand, you may also wonder as to why 'water' was included in the above as one of the iconic values of the logogram i**ru**.

The basic Dravidian root for 'water' is **nīr** (நீர்); in my opinion it is dentalized derivative of **īr** (ஈர்) *'wet, watery'*. The reader will be better equipped to keep pace with this book if he always bears in mind the following guideline:

Guideline 14 *Several Dravidian words beginning with a dental consonant **n** or **t** occurred de-dentalized in the Harappan, that is, without the initial dental consonant.*

*For example, **naṅkai** (நங்கை) lady', **taṅkai** (தங்கை) younger sister' was **aṅkai** (அங்கை) in Harappan, with relevant identified sign*  and

nampi *(நம்பி) 'gentleman',* ***tampi*** *(தம்பி) 'younger brother' was* ***ampi /ampay*** *(அம்பி / அம்பை) in Harappan, with relevant identified sign* 

<u>Guideline 15</u> *A few of the Harappan words with initial dental consonant* ***t*** *or* ***n*** *dropped it while passing over to the Dravidian vocabulary. For example,* ***nāl*** *(நால்) meaning 'rope' or 'fibre' or 'banyan-tree' or instrumental case (third case) postposition 'by, with' became* ***āl*** *(ஆல்).*

The word **iru** (இரு) occurs hundreds of times in Sangam Literature in the sense of **'great', 'large', 'huge', 'divine', 'authoritative'** etc. We should distinguish it from the word for **big.**

peru (பெரு) means **'big'.**

Iru (இரு) means **'great' / 'divine'.**

The term 'irunkō (இருங்கோ)' which occurs in Classical Tamil literary works means **'great king';** it occurs in Harappan writing as:

 or 

In fact, this **iru** (இரு) became the famous *'honorific title'* **tiru** (திரு) in Dravidian Languages.

10.02 The **iru** sign is comparable to the Mesopotamian divinity sign **AN**

In Sumerian Language, **diĝir** or **dingir**(திங்கிர்) means **God** and it is called **AN** in Akkadian and other Mesopotamian languages.

Whenever names of gods, deities, angels etc. are to be mentioned, invariably this divinity sign is added in front. However, the sign is only a ***semantic indicator***, informing the reader that the word which follows is of divine nature, hence **it is not pronounced.**

The convention was so rigidly followed that even when you mention the generic name **god,** you have to write it as **diĝir diĝir.** Here also, the first **diĝir** used as indicator is **not** pronounced.

In what follows, <u>unpronounced portions are shown in brackets.</u>

𒀭 = **diĝir**

𒀭𒀭 = (**diĝir**) **diĝir** *'the God'*

ENKI is the god living in the sub-terrestrial world, responsible for experience, magic, sedition etc.

𒀭𒂗𒆠 = (**diĝir**) **EN-KI**

ENLIL is head of gods / angels, almost similar to our Indra.

𒀭𒂗𒆤 = (**diĝir**) **EN-LIL**

DAMU is the God of good Health and healer of all ailments / diseases, similar to our puranic ***Dhanvantari,*** *the God of Ayurveda.*

𒀭𒁕𒈬 = (**diĝir**) **DAMU**

The situation in Harappan Language is nearly the same. The **iru** sign serves as the *divinity sign* and it is also **not** pronounced but there is a structural difference. The **iru** sign ***<u>follows</u>*** the logogram it qualifies, that is, it is placed after the logogram.

We have learnt that:

 = **el** (எல்) ***'sun'***, **pāl** (பால்) *'milk, white'*, **pakal** (பகல்) *'daytime'*, **nāḷ** (நாள்) *'day'* ', **veyil** (வெயில்) ***'sunshine'***, **veḷiccam** வெளிச்சம் ***'light'.***

Let us now add divinity sign and upper class ending **an**,

 = *(god)* **ellan (எல்லன்),** *(god)* **pakalōn, (பகலோன்). Denotes Sun-God; the divinity sign**  *(god) is not to be pronounced.*

Please see the following inscriptions:

 **2697 -11 -1**

 **3505 -11 -2**

If you put in some extra efforts, you can interpret the second inscription.

 = *(god)* **ellappanār (எல்லப்பனார்)** ***'Sun God'***

10.03 We have earlier seen that

 = **maḻai** (மழை) *'rain'*, **māri (**மாரி) *'deadly disease, small pox'*, **iruḷ** (இருள்) *'darkness'*

When we add the divinity sign, we get:

 = *(god)* **maḻai** (மழை) *'rain god'*, (later on **varuṇa**)

Look at the following document:

 **1273 -11 -1**

13.04 when we pinch out one edge stroke from **ma<u>l</u>ai** sign we get,

 = **munai, muni, nuni** (முனை, முனி, நுனி) ***'edge'.***

When we add here the divinity indicator sign, we get:

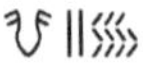 = *(god)* **munian** (முனியன்)

This is a popular and important village deity in Tamil Nadu; it is held in so high esteem and reverence in the South Hindu pantheon that **īśvara** (ஈஸ்வர) title is added to the name of deity as **munīśvaran** (முனீஸ்வரன்). There are ample reasons to believe that this deity was also quite popular in the Indus Valley, particularly in Harappa. Inscriptions containing the name of this deity occur aplenty and usually with the honorific plural ending **ār** (ஆர்).

 = **(god** கடவுள்) **muniyanār**

(முனியனார்) Scrutinize the following inscriptions:

 **4094 -22 -1**

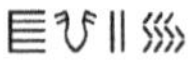 **4444 -22 -2**

 **4456 -22 -3**

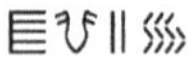 **4472 -2 -22 -4**

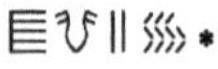 **4481 -2 -22 -5**

 **4563 -22 -6**

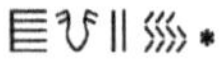 **4581 -2 -22 -7**

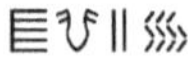 **5401 -2 -22 -8**

 **5485 -2 -22 -9**

 **5486 -2 -22 -10**

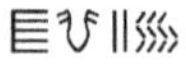 **5498 -22 -11**

11. Murukā...Ammā...Murukā...

11.01 Usually, people invoke Lord Muruga with the expression ***Murukā...Appā...Murukā*** (முருகா...அப்பா...முருகா). Hence, the ***caption*** may look weird, but you'll shortly find it meaningful. One of most frequently occurring complex signs that you meet in the Indus Inscriptions is *intersecting circles* or *intersecting ovals.*

In fact, both the kinds occurred at the beginning of the Indus writing,

; but in course of time with the sole aim of avoiding confusion*, the intersecting circle sign was merged with the intersecting oval sign*.

This sign is so important that the pioneering Indus Scholar, Asko Parpola has included a complete chapter to deal with the sign in his *chef-d'œuvre,* **'Deciphering the Indus Script'** *vide* chapter 13 *Evidence for Harappan Worship of the god Muruku.*

Though Iravatham Mahadevan held initially a view differing from Asko Parpola regarding the interpretation of the sign for Lord Muruga, it seems that he has later become compromised with the other's viewpoint.

When we add the divinity sign with each of them, we get names of two important Gods.

Using intersecting ovals we get,

= amman (அம்மன்) *'Mother God'*

Using intersecting circles we get,

= muruku + an (முரு + அன்) >> **muruvan** (முருவன்) >> **murukan** (முருகன்)

As already pointed out, in the course of time with the sole aim of avoiding confusion, both the signs merged together as intersecting ovals only and the _intersecting circles were given up_. Even though confusion in the figures of the signs has gone, a new confusion between the Gods, **Amman** and **Murukan** has cropped up. The scholarly assembly devising a script to Harappan Language, has decided to put an end to this problem also.

11.02 The name of Mother God begins with the vowel **'a'**, hence it was felt that there is <u>no need</u> for any extra sign for phonetic indication:

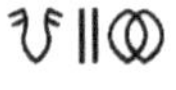 = **amman** (அம்மன்) *'Mother God'*

However, some extra-cautious scribes sometimes added the **a<u>r</u>am** sign  which serves as short vowel **'a',** in order to emphasize the fact that the word in question begins with the vowel sound **'a'**. It is unpronounced.

	= **amman** (அம்மன்) *'Mother God'*

11.03 Coming to Lord Muruga, they have decided to add a phonetic indicator '¦' = **mu,** a ***special*** three-stroke sign differing from the usual numeral sign for three III.

	= **murukan** (முருகன்) *'Lord Muruga'*

Please note that the special three-stroke sign chosen by Indus Scholars bears resemblance to the triangular country oven used in Indian households in those days with the name **chūl** (சூல்) *'oven';* but this word has a homonym meaning **pregnancy** and Lord Muruga is considered to be the Protector God of women's pregnancy.

Please see:

 **4477 -22 -1**

However, the Indus Scribes adhering sincerely to their ***minimality principle,*** tried to omit the divinity sign || whenever the sign '¦' is used as phonetic indicator, feeling that the special sign may also be considered as a semantic indicator for **godliness.** There are in all not less than **19** instances:

 **1257 -11 -1**

 **1366 -11 -2**

 **1529 -11 -3**

 **1530 -11 -4**

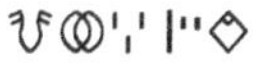 **3039 -11 -5**

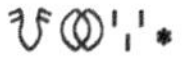 **4363 -22 -6**

 **4512 -22 -7**

 **4519 -22 -8**

 **4553 -22 -9**

 **4554 -22 -10**

 **4555 -22 -11**

 **4564 -22 -12**

 **4629 -22 -13**

 **4651 -22 -14**

 **5250 -22 -15**

 **5308 -22 -16**

 **5452 -22 -17**

 **5470 -22 -18**

 **7035 -44 -19**

Among them, 5 inscriptions (3, 4, 8, 14, 16) occur with additional *respect plural particle* **ār** so that the expression may be pronounced as **murukanār** (முருகனார்).

In the above list, since item No.5 contains additionally one single stroke the **oru** stroke, it may be presumed that the expression is not meant for invocation of Lord Muruga, but to denote the name of a person called 'murukan'.

 = A person bearing the name **Murukan** (முருகன்).

On the other hand, there are about 6 (six) instances where the logogram for God,  **iṟai** (இறை) is used instead of the **cūl** sign 

 = (God) **murukan** (முருகன்) *'Lord Muruga'*

 **1077 -11 -1**

 **1629 -11 -2**

 **2252 -11 -3**

 **2863 -11 -4**

 **4263 -22 -5**

 **6306 -2 -33 -6**

Apart from the above list, the occurrence of  would denote **amman**:

 **1146 -11 -1**

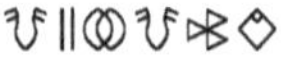 **1215 -11 -2**

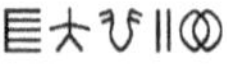 **1227 -2 -11 -3**

 **1369 -11 -4**

 **1536 -11 -5**

 **1541 -11 -6**

 **1628 -11 -7**

 **2115 -11 -8**

 **2246 -11 -9**

 **4253 -22 -10**

 **4271 -22 -12**

 **4306 -22 -13**

 **4306 -2 -22 -14**

 **4427 -2 -22 -15**

 **4658 -2 -22 -16**

 **5324 -2 -22 -17**

 **5474 -22 -18**

 **6229 -33 -19**

 **6306 -2 -33 -20**

 **7097 -44 -21**

Note: In the above inscriptions, the divinity sign ||, **the** phonetic indicator  and the godly / royal determinative  are ***not to be pronounced.*** Hence, we may understand that the Indus people were ***quite clear*** as to which God they referred to in the inscriptions.

In so far as the Harappans are concerned, **amman** is **amman** and **murukan** is **murukan;** there is utterly **no** confusion.

 **= amman (அம்மன்)**

 **= murukan (முருகன்)**

We will follow the above convention throughout this book.

12. *Two-Stroke as Urban-Stroke*

12.01 In Mesopotamia, the names of cities and other urban areas are invariably affixed with the city determinative **iri** or **uru.**

 = **iri** or **uru** ('இரி' / 'உரு)

We also know that in the Indus Script, the two-stroke is pronounced as **iru** or **iri** meaning **two** in the Harappan Language. Further, we have already seen that this **iru** meaning *'great'* became later the important **tiru** (திரு) in the Dravidian Languages and the association of the particle **tiru** with city / place name is also well known. In a way, the particle **tiru** may be considered as ***place-name builder***.

12.02 When you add **tiru** with **malai** meaning *'mountain', you get* ***tirumalai*** (திருமலை), the name of a town.

When you add **tiru** with **aṇṇā malai** meaning *'elder brother mountain', you get* ***tiruvaṇṇamalai*** (திருவண்ணாமலை), the name of a town.

When you add **tiru** with **ai** (ஐ) **āṟu** (ஆறு) meaning *'five rivers', you get* ***tiruvaiyāṟu*** (திருவையாறு), the name of a town.

When you add **tiru (തിരു)** with **valla (വല്ല)** meaning *'basket boat'*, you get ***tiruvalla (തിരുവല്ല)***, the name of a town in Kerala.

When you add **tiru (திரு)** with **valli kēṇi** meaning *'well with creepers'*, you get ***tiruvallikēṇi*** (திருவல்லிகேணி), the name of a suburb in Chennai.

There are hundreds of such names of towns in South India in general, Tamil Nadu and Kerala in particular.

As we know, the phonetic value of the two-sign || is **iru / iri** as in Mesopotamia and it was also used in Harappan Land as <u>a determinative for town or place name</u>. Unlike in present day South India, this particle was ***not pronounced*** in Harappa as in Mesopotamia.

Here is a thumb rule to identify such determinative.

<u>Guideline 16</u> *In the Indus Script inscriptions, whenever the two-sign ||*

(a) *is **not** part of the complex sign for long **ā,*** 
(b) *is **not** a sign explicitly indicating the numeral **two***
(c) *is **not** used as **divinity determinative,***

*then it indicates **town** or **placename**.*

<u>Guideline 17</u> *Out of the several values of a logogram, one will be the principal value. Normally, the value for which the logogram was originally devised will be the principal value. This principal value is considered as the **default value** of the logogram, for which no additional sign is required as phonetic / semantic indicator or determinative to pinpoint that meaning or value. Hence, in order to indicate the default value of a logogram, the same can be written without any entourage and it can occur alone.*

The following example will make the point clearer.

 = **nakar** (நகர்), **ūr** (ஊர்), **paḷḷi** (பள்ளி), **'pāḻi'** (பாழி), **nāṭu** (நாடு) etc...

There is a similar sign with almost the <u>*same meanings*</u> in the Egyptian Hieroglyphic, .

I feel that the origin of **nakar** (நகர்) is **4**, namely, **nāl** (நால்), **nālu** (நாலு, **nān** (நான்), **nānku** (நான்கு). Our sign is associated with the words, **nānilam** (நானிலம்) *'country' literally meaning the four lands of Tamil Tradition,* **ñālam** (ஞாலம்) *'Earth' or World'*

The city area where upper class people lived (மேட்டுக் குடியினர் வாழுமிடம்) was called **mēl / mēṭu** (மேல் / மேடு) otherwise called the CITADEL and it is denoted by the sign  and the area where <u>*the others lived was*</u> called **nāṭu** (நாடு) and denoted by the sign ; it is related to **four** (4); you can note the four quarters in the sign.

In fact, both the words **nakar** (நகர்), and **nāṭu** (நாடு) originated from the numeric word **nālu** (நாலு), hence the term **nakar** is the principal or default value. When we use the sign  in this sense, <u>it is not necessary to add any indicator or determinative and it is enough to use the sign alone.</u>

Suppose the Indus Valley Harappans wanted to use the sign in the sense of **ūr** (ஊர்), then following the Mesopotamian practice they added the city determinative **iru / iri,** namely the two-stroke ||.

 || = **ūr** (ஊர்) *'town'*

12.03 Before going to the next topic, let us now examine a few illustrative examples.

(a)  = **'āvūr'** (ஆவூர்). One of the prominent contributors to the anthologies of Tamil Sangam Literature was **āvūr**

kiḻār (ஆவூர் கிழார்). There are more than one **āvūr** (ஆவூர்) in Tamil Nadu.

Real time example from Indus Inscriptions:

 **4095 -22**

The corrupted sign  at the end is probably  and the inscription may be read as **'āvūran'** (ஆவூரன்)

(b)  = **iṟaiyūr /eṟaiyūr** (இறையூர் / எறையூர்).

There are several **iṟaiyūr /eṟaiyūr** (இறையூர் / எறையூர்) in Tamil Nadu today; one near Chennai, and one near Neyveli etc.

Look at the following inscription:

 **2321 -11**

In this inscription  is found a bit corrupted; the inscription as a whole is to be read as **iṟaiyūran /eṟaiyūran** (இறையூரன் / எறையூரன்), a person hailing from **iṟaiyūr / eṟaiyūr** (இறையூர் / எறையூர்) as we say New-Yorker, Londoner or Parisian.

(c) 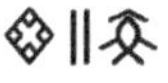 = **'uṟaiyūr' /'oṟaiyūr'** (உறையூர் / ஒறையூர்)

There is still a **uṟaiyūr;** it is a suburb of metropolitan Trichy or Tiruchirapalli in Tamil Nadu. For several centuries in the first millennium CE, **uṟaiyūr** was capital of Chola Empire in South India. Attestations in Indus inscriptions are as follows:

 **2406 -11**

 **9022 -66**

The portion marked red (or greyed) in the first inscription and the whole of the second inscription are to be read as **uṟaiyūran / oṟaiyūran** (உறையூரன் / ஒறையூரன்), a person hailing from **uṟaiyūr / oṟaiyūr** (உறையூர் / ஒறையூர்) as in the case of (b) above.

From time immemorial, communal harmony was maintained in South Asian society through democratic arbitration by a five-member committee consisting of persons of importance, known as ***Panchayat***. We had **village panchayat, town panchayat, city panchayat** etc. depending on the size of human habitation in a place.

Panchayat was called **aincavai** in Harappan civilization. **aincavai** is a compound word made of:

aincu (ஐஞ்சு) *'five'* + **avai** (அவை) *'assembly / committee'*= **aincavai** (ஐஞ்சவை) *'panchayat'*

Member of a panchayat was called **aincan** (ஐஞ்சன்)

In the Indus Script:

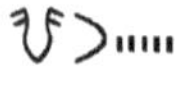 = **aincan** (ஐஞ்சன்)

Please peruse the inscription discovered in Mohenjodaro:

 **Inscription No. 1311-11**

I read the above as **nakar aincan** (நகர் ஐஞ்சன்) *'town panchayat member'*

12.04 Another important and frequently occurring human sign is:

a human figure carrying a pole or **yoke** (*'a frame fitted to a person's shoulders to carry a load in two equal portions'* as per Merriam-Webster dictionary) on the shoulders, from the two edges of which hang two bundles of load, one on either edge. It is similar to a person carrying a traditional ***kāvaṭi*** (காவடி). To denote a load or burden there are two words of import, *viz.,* **poṟai** (பொறை), **poti** (பொதி)

As we have seen earlier, a logogram denotes not only its iconic meaning but also its associated concepts***, verbs and personae***. Hence,  = (substantives) **poṟai** *(பொறை)*, **poti** *(பொதி)*, load, burden, responsibility, ***kāvaṭi*** *(காவடி) and* associated verbs)

poṟu *(பொறு)* - 'bear', 'sustain'; **tāṅku** *(தாங்கு)* – 'bear', 'hold'; **tūkku** *(தூக்கு)* – 'lift'; **māṭṭu** *(மாட்டு)* – 'to fasten on', 'to hook', 'hang', etc; **cuma** *(சும)* – 'be burdened', 'carry a burden'; and also the associated personae:

poṟai *(பொறை)* – 'bearer', 'official'; **poṟaiyan** *(பொறையன்)* – 'officer'

The sign  is named as **poṟai** *(பொறை).*

From the above several meanings, I cull out a single one for further discussions; this corresponds to DEDR entry No.4802. The reason why I have specifically culled out this item is that this sign is extended by **metonymy** to a ***postposition*** of importance,

māṭṭu *(மாட்டு)* – ***'for', 'for the sake of', 'on account of'***

This postposition has in later days been replaced by 'kāva (kāga)', 'kōcaram (ōcaram)' in Tamil, 'kōsaramu', 'kōsamu' in Telugu *vide.* DEDR entry No.871.

This postposition occurs **14** times in **tirukkuṟal** *(திருக்குறள்)* as in

துன்னியார் குற்றமும் தூற்றும் மரபினார்
என்னைகொல் ஏதிலார் **மாட்டு**. 188

It occurs about **18** times in **eṭṭu-tokai** *(எட்டு-தொகை)* – 'eight anthologies' of the ancient Tamil Sangam Literature as in

வெறுத்த ஏஎர், வேய்புரை பணைத் தோள்,

நிறுப்ப நில்லா நெஞ்சமொடு நின் **மாட்டு**

இவளும், இனையள் ஆயின் ...

-akam-nānūṟu *(அகம்-நானூறு)* -**'Mind-400'**

There is another reason as to why I give specific preference to this interpretation. For the meaning under discussion, the Hindi/Urdu postposition is **'ke liye',** but in Gujarati spoken in the heartland of - Indus Valley, it is **māṭe** (માટે):

Hindi / Urdu	Gujarati
के लिए	માટે
ke liye	māṭē

Occurrence of such Dravidian elements in the core structure of west Indian languages is not surprising; in fact, we'll be discussing a similar situation in Punjabi in a later chapter. In view of the above consideration, I have chosen to ascribe this phonetic value to the human sign under consideration which very frequently occurs as the word-final element:

 = (post-position) **māṭṭu** *(மாட்டு)*

Similarly, throughout this book we read the following expressions as indicated:

 = **poṟai** (பொறை) *'person-in-charge, official'*

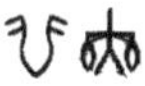 = **poṟaiyan** (பொறையன்) *'officer'*

 = **poṟaiyār** (பொறையார்) *'mayor'*

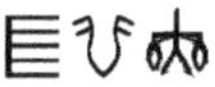 = **poṟaiyanār** (பொறையனார்) 'administrator'

Now, we can read the following inscription from Mohenjodaro.

 = **nakar poṟaiyār** (நகர் பொறையார்) *'city mayor'* 2289-11

We have seen earlier that the **iru** stroke || placed next to a logogram, adds sanctity / divinity or **authority** to the meaning of the logogram. With this point in mind let us read the following inscription also from Mohenjodaro:

 = **nakar āṭci** (நகராட்சி) *(town administration or Municipality)* 2579-11

Adding the two-stroke divinity sign to  which means government, governance, rule, ruler etc. endows certain sanctity or authority to the logogram. Whenever it is used to denote King ('வேந்து', 'அரசு', 'மன்னன்') the authority sign is invariably added as 

13. *Three-Stroke*

13.01 Another versatile stroke-sign occurring in the Indus Script is the **three-stroke** ||| and we have already learnt how an important determinative it is in Harappan writing. We have seen that this determinative placed after a logogram specifies that some ***verbal action*** is associated with the logogram, and we have got also acquainted with some of its applications. We are now going to study this sign in depth in this chapter.

First of all, we'll give the sign a name. Its basic phonetic value is **mu** but there is another variant 'ı' which is exclusively used for phonetic value **mu** and associated with Lord Muruga. Hence, we may call that variant sign as 'ı' **mu** (மு) sign. For reasons to be explained later we may call the three-sign as **mutu** (முது) sign. The following phonetic convention in interpreting the signs of the Indus Script are worth remembering.

*<u>**Guideline 018**</u> The phonetic value of any sign **ending in a vowel** sound is automatically extendable to cover the cases of the sign **plus** the **unrepresented** suffixes,* **tu** (து) *and* **ttu** (த்து)

<u>Examples:</u>

1. The phonetic value of the sign  **'a'** is automatically extendable to **atu** (அது) and **attu** (அத்து); in fact, the demonstrative substantives **itu, atu, utu** and the interrogative **etu** are simply default extensions of their classical counterparts **a, i, u** and **e.**

2. The phonetic value of the sign  **'eḻu'** (எழு) *'seven'* is automatically extendable to **eḻutu** (எழுது) *'to write'* and **eḻuttu** (எழுத்து) *'letter'.*

3. The phonetic value of the sign ||| **'mu'** (மு) *'syllable **mu**'* is automatically extendable to **mu*t*u** (முது) *'old, senior'* and **mu*tt*u** (முத்து) *'pearl'*.

After all these discussions, we can understand why the name of the three-sign ||| was given as **mutu** (முது).

13.02 Sometimes, the determinative, **mutu** instead of occurring as a separate sign, merges with the logogram in question to form a complex sign. We have earlier studied the sign of intersecting circles  meaning **muruku** and the sign of intersecting ovals  meaning **amma.** The determinative **mutu** merges with each of the above overlapping signs so as to form two different complex signs:

The first complex sign  with strokes marked in slant position denotes verbal actions associated with ***'mother'*** and the second complex sign  with strokes marked in vertical position denotes verbal actions associated with Lord ***Murukan***.

Verbal activities associated with **mother** conceived by the Harappan Scholars are:

pe<u>r</u>u பெறு (குழந்தை பெறுதல்) 'to give birth'.

pi<u>r</u>a பிற (குழந்தையாகப் பிறத்தல்) 'to be born'.

pēṇu பேணு (பேணி வளர்த்தல்) 'to rear children'.

pe<u>r</u>u பெறு (அடைதல், பெறுதல்) 'to receive'.

pēṟu பேறு (பாக்கியம்) ‘’boon’

Further, phonetic syllables derived therefrom are:

pe (பெ), **pi** (பி), **pē** (பே), **pī** (பீ)

Hence,

 = **piṟa** (பிற), **peṟu** (பெறு), **pēṟu** (பேறு), **பேணு;**

pe (பெ), **pi** (பி), **pē** (பே), **pī** (பீ)

Let us now see an interesting example frequently occurring in the Indus Inscriptions:

 = **pē** (பே)

 = **ri** (ரி)

 = **kai** (கை)

 = **pērikai** (பேரிகை, முரசு) *'drum'*

This expression occurs about 17 times in the Indus Inscriptions from different areas of excavation.

 **1709 -11 -1**

 **2903 -2 -11 -2**

The first inscription can be read as **nal iṟai pēṟikai** (நல் இறை பேரிகை) *'benevolent Royal Drum'.* Here **iṟai** is used in the sense of **'royal'.**

The second one is a grammatically important example; we'll be dealing with this example shortly in detail.

13.03 What about the intersecting circles with three small vertical strokes purported to be associated with Lord **Muruka**?

What are the specific verbal actions connected with Lord **Muruka**? From religious point of view, the verbal action which stands out is:

 = **veṟiyāṭu** (வெறியாடு) *'dance in trance under possession by Muruga'*

Dancing in trance in Muruga temples is called **veṟiyāṭu** (வெறியாடு) and the dance itself is called **veṟiyāṭṭam** (வெறியாட்டம்) (முருகன் கோவில்களில் **'அருள்'** வந்து ஆடுதலை **'வெறியாடுதல்'**, **'வெறியாட்டம்'** என்பர்) References abound in Sangam and later old Tamil Literature.

Let us now come back to the example:

 **2903 -2 -11**

13.04 When we want to refer to a non-descript person, we usually say a ***'gentleman'***; and if it is a woman, we say a ***'lady'***. The equivalent words in Harappan Language are ***ambi** (later **nambi**) and* ***ankai** (later **nankai**).*

Hence, the two signs and serve **also** as ***class-indicators***, the first as *upper-class indicator* and the second as *non-class indicator*.

Sometimes, these two signs serve not simply as passive ***class-indicators*** but also as active **class-makers.** Please bear in mind that *feminine* is included in *non-class*. The following examples will make my views clearer.

The famous archaic musical instrument very frequently referred to in Sangam Literature as **yāḻ** (யாழ்) has a compulsive semantic or synonymous extension to *'song or poem'*.

 = **yāḻ** (யாழ்) *'ancient musical instrument'*, **pāṇ** (பாண்) *'song, poem'*

When we add the universal upper-class ending , we get:

 = **pāṇan** (பாணன்) *'singer'* / **pulavan** (புலவன்) *'poet'*

Add further the **class maker** or **class-modifier** sign to get:

 = *feminine* **pāṇan** (*பெண்பால்* பாணன்) *'female singer'* / *feminine* **pulavan** (பெண்பால் புலவன்) *'female poet or poetess'*

The sign  occurring as initial element in a word or expression is most likely the **class-modifier.** It indicates that the explicit class of the expression which follows the sign has to be changed. Here is a classic example which would go a long way to illustrate the concept of **class-modifier.**

13.05 In the Harappan language, the word **ancal** (அஞ்சல்) means *'news'* or *'message'* and **ancan** (அஞ்சன்) denotes *'newsman or announcer of news'* usually by beating the drum 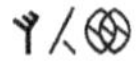 = **pērikai** (பேரிகை) *'tom-tom, drum'*:

 = *phonetic syllable* **am** (அம்)

 = *phonetic syllable* **-ca-** (-ச-)

 = *universal upper-class ending serving also as the phonetic syllable* **-an** (-அன்)

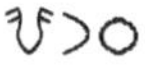 **= anca-an >> ancan** (அஞ்சன்) *'announcer / messenger / newsman'*

Let us now watch the effect of adding the class-modifier  which converts the ***upper-class noun into non-class one***.

 **= ancal** (அஞ்சல்) *'announcement / messenge / news'*

Let us now try to interpret the whole expressions:

 **= pērikai-ancan** (பேரிகை-அஞ்சன்) *'drum announcer'*

If we add the sign  **the non-class modifier** (அஃறிணைத் திணை-மாற்றி) we get:

 **= pērikai-ancal** (பேரிகை-அஞ்சல்) *'drum announcement / drum-news'*

In a similar fashion the sign  also serves as **upper-class-modifier**, however, the necessity therefor seldom arises.

14. *Biliteral Consonant Combos*

14.01 There are in all 18 consonants in Classical Tamil, and they are divided into three groups with six consonants each.

(1) **Hard : k, c, ṭ, t, p, ṟ** (வல்லினம் : க், ச், ட், த், ப், ற்)

(2) **Soft: ṅ, ñ, ṇ, n, m, ṉ** (மெல்லினம் : ங், ஞ், ண், ந், ம், ன்)

(3) **Medial : y, r, l, v, ḻ, ḷ** (இடையினம் : ய், ர், ல், வ், ழ், ள்)

Out of these 18 consonants, with the exception of **r (ர்)** and **ḻ** (*ழ்)* all others ***can occur as double consonants***

kk, cc, ṭṭ, tt, pp, ṟṟ (க்க, ச்ச, ட்ட, த்த, ப்ப, ற்ற)

ṅṅ, ññ, ṇṇ, nn, mm, ṉṉ (ங்ங, ஞ்ஞ, ண்ண, ந்ந, ம்ம, ன்ன)

yy, ll, vv, ḷḷ (ய்ய, ல்ல, வ்வ, ள்ள)

*In my opinion each of the above double consonants **has a separate sign** in the **Indus Script**; we have to only identify them.*

The **18** consonants would give rise to **18 X 18 = 324** possible ***biliteral consonant pairs*** including the 16 double consonants already discussed. <u>Do we need separate signs for all these **324** consonant combos?</u> The answer is an emphatic **NO**. Why?

Tamil enshrines some kind of **phonetic orthodoxy** in relation to positional use of consonants. ***Among the major world languages,* Tamil *<u>uses the least number of biliteral consonant combos</u>.***

We have seen that there may be **324** possible biliteral phonetic syllables in Tamil, *but in actual practice only **a very small fraction** of possible biliteral combos occur.*

Tamil Grammarians use a technical term **mey mayakkam** (மெய் மயக்கம்) to deal with the cases of biliteral consonant combos.

For example, consider **k** (க்) one of the 18 consonants. Theoretically speaking, it can be followed by 18 consonants *<u>including itself</u>* to form 18 biliteral ***combos*** as detailed below:

kk, kṅ, kc, kñ, kṭ, kṇ, (க்க், க்ங், க்ச், க்ஞ், க்ட், க்ண்),

kt, kn, kp, km, ky, kr, (க்த், க்ந், க்ப், க்ம், க்ய், க்ர்),

kl, kv, kḻ, kḷ, kṟ, kṉ, (க்ல், க்வ், க்ழ், க்ள், க்ற், க்ன்)

Out of the above 18 biliteral combos **only one** *is used in Tamil and the remaining* ***17 are prohibited or ruled out.***

So, we need only one sign for ***kk. It is already there:*** 

14.02 Similarly, consider **p** (ப்) one of the 18 consonants. Theoretically speaking, it can be followed by 18 consonants *including itself* to form 18 biliteral syllables as indicated below:

pk, pṅ, pc, pñ, pṭ, pṇ, (ப்க், ப்ங், ப்ச், ப்ஞ், ப்ட், ப்ண்),

pt, pn, pp, pm, py, pr, (ப்த், ப்ந், **ப்ப்**, ப்ம், ப்ய், ப்ர்),

pl, pv, pḻ, pḷ, pṟ, pṉ, (ப்ல், ப்வ், ப்ழ், ப்ள், ப்ற், ப்ன்)

Out of the above 18 biliteral combos **only one** *is used in Tamil and the remaining* ***17 are prohibited or ruled out.***

So, we need only one sign for ***pp. It is already there:*** 

14.03 In the same manner, each of the remaining 16 consonants generate only **a very few** biliteral consonant combos.

Even though all grammatical works in Classical Tamil are posterior to Harappan period, the closest to Harappan is **tolkāppiyam.**

If we take stock of all biliteral consonant combos authorised by **tolkāppiyam,** only about **80 combos** stand out**. Hence,** we'll need only about **80** *mixed biliteral signs to take complete care* of bilateral requirements of the Harappan Language.

Let us now analyse the biliteral consonant combos in question. There are **16** double consonants amongst them, and we have already discovered signs for **12**:

1.  = **kk (க்க)**
2.  = **cc (ச்ச)**
3.  = **pp (ப்ப)**
4.  = **mm (ம்ம)**

5.  = **ṉṉ (ன்ன)**

6.  = **yy (ய்ய)**

7.  = **ṭṭ (ட்ட)**

8.  or  = **ṟṟ (ற்ற)**

9.  **= tt (த்த)**

10.  **= vv (வ்வ)**

11.  **= ḷḷ (ள்ள)**

12.  **= ll (ல்ல)**

Coming to mixed consonant pairs, we have hitherto positively identified only the following 4:

1  = **mp (ம்ப்)**

2  = **ṅk ங்க்**

3  = **ṇṭ ண்ட்**

4  = **ṉṟ ன்ற்**

We are yet to discover about 60 consonant pairs of mixed type.

Truly speaking, we have not paid due attention towards this end. In fact, there are some easily discernible pairs. In Tamil, **l (ல்)** followed by a surd becomes **ṟ (ற்)** and  is the sign for **la**

 = **l + kay > ṟ + kay** (e.g. **iyaṟkay** இயற்கை *'nature')*

 = **l + ku > ṟ + ku** (e.g. **teṟku** தெற்கு *'south')*

 = **l + pa > ṟ + pa** (e.g. **kaṟpanai** கற்பனை *'imagination')*

 = **l + paṭu > ṟ + paṭu** (e.g. **muṟpaṭu** முற்படு *'try, take effort')*

They are respectively sign combos:

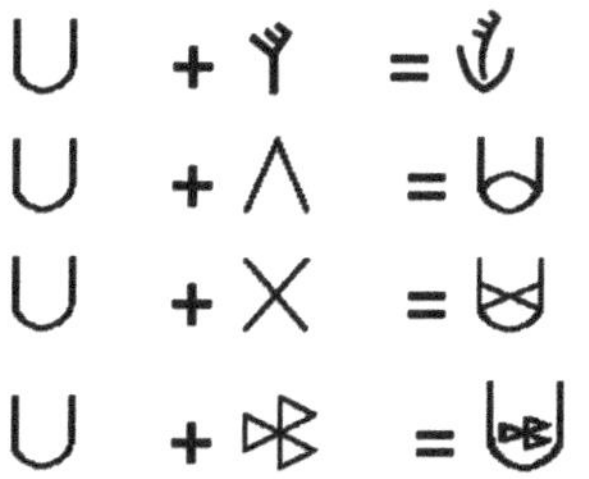

14.04 Furthermore, consonants with the inherent short vowel **a** sound is the order of the day in South Asian Scripts as **ka** (க), **ca** (ச), **ta** (த) etc. we may consider them as appellation. Suppose we have a logogram whose phonetic value contains some consonant, for which no sign has so far been prescribed, the vowel sound with which it occurs is ignored and the logogram is adopted as ***phonetic syllable for that consonant*** and called with an "**a**" sound.

For example, we have a logogram to denote rain,  **maḻai** (மழை) *'rain'* and it is used as phonetic syllable **ḻa** (ழ) as well as **ḻai** (ழை).

Another classical example that we are about to deal with will certainly be quite illustrative in this regard. From the picture, the following sign is interpreted as 'guard', 'security' etc.

 = **kāval** (காவல்)

The first syllable of the word is culled out and prescribed as the phonetic syllable **kā** (கா).

Hence, we have:

 = *logogram* **kāval** (காவல்) *'guard. Security',*

Phonetic syllable **kā** (கா).

Look at the picture: a man is holding a long stick or pole. The pole sign or the one-sign is used in some complex signs for ***elongation*** of the vowel sound. Logically, removal of such stick sign from a complex sign should introduce ***shortening*** of the vowel sound; am I correct? So, if we omit the stick portion from our sign, we should get the short vowel sound:

 = **ka** (க).

15. Consonant Combos

15.01 A study of complex signs formed in the Indus Script with the help of two or more simple signs has revealed that the Harappans never gave up their aesthetic sense and their proclivity towards symmetry; the ***Harappan touch is commendable***.

When two simple signs join together, they add a small stroke, like forward slash, on the right or a backlash on the left or both forward and back lashes on either side or a vertical stroke.

(a) Forward slash / on the right:

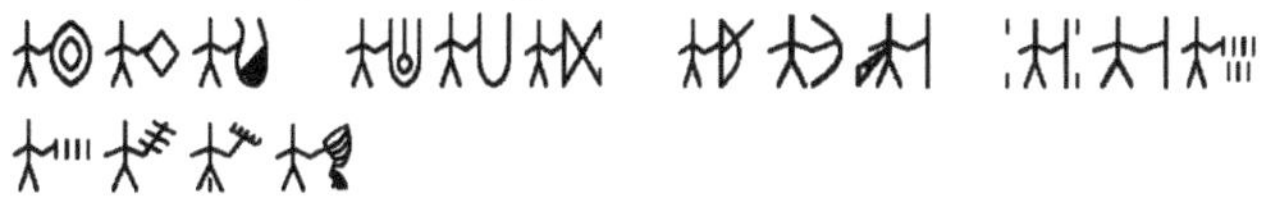

(b) Back slash \ on the right:

(c) Forward slash / on the left:

( **is = | +** )

(d) One forward slash / on the right and one backslash \ on the left:

(e) Vertical stroke | between the constituents:

( is =  + )

15.02 We must also try to distinguish between the two signs:

 and 

The complex sign  is a combination of the 'human' **āḷ** sign  and the 'bow-arrow' **vill-ampu** sign,  while  is a combination of human sign and double the 'bow-arrow sign'.

Similar is the case with  which is a combination of the 'human' **āḷ** sign  and double the 'pole' **kōl** sign, whereas,

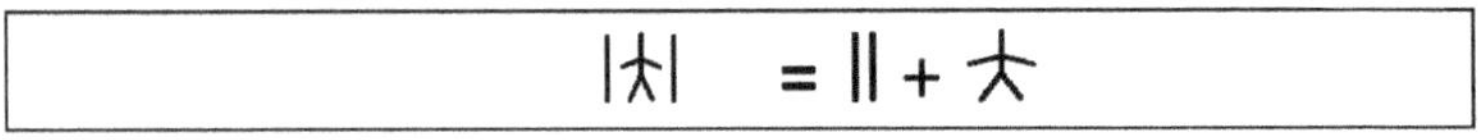

15.03 To tell you the truth, I have my own theory about these simple and complex signs. In fact, I feel that this is the right place to share my own theory with the reader so that both of us could be on the same network or wavelength.

In the early stage of the Harappan writing system, the verbs associated with human activities were represented by a combo of human sign and related noun sign. In course of time, the Harappan scholars felt that the ***noun sign itself*** could be used for related verbal action also; hence the human sign which became redundant was dropped.

For example, we have already met the **kalam** sign,  with the interpretation as **vessel, cup, tumbler**. Initially, when the Harappans wanted to mean a verb associated with **kalam,** they added a human sign  and formed a complex sign  to denote **'to drink'.** However, in course of time, they dropped the human sign and used the **kalam** sign  alone to mean the verb**, 'to drink'.**

15.04 Whenever two simple signs combine together to form a complex sign, any of the three things happen as given in the following guideline:

***<u>Guideline 010</u>*** *Whenever two simple signs combine to form a single **complex** sign,*

(1) if <u>one of the component sign is bigger than the other</u> in size, then the convention of reading requires that the

bigger sign should be read first followed by the smaller one;

e.g.

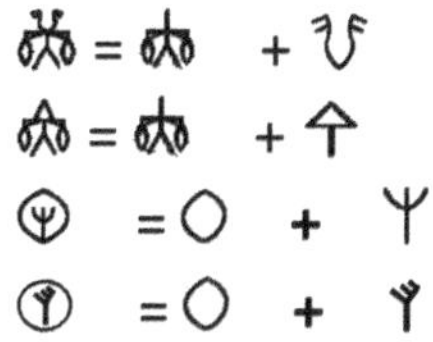

(2) *If both the components are of the <u>same size and occur side by side</u>, then the right-side sign should be read first and the left-side sign next;*

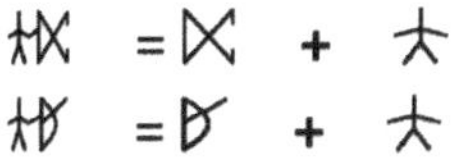

(3) *If both the components are of the <u>same size</u> and occur <u>one above the other</u>, then the upper sign should be read first and the lower sign next.*

15.05 Let us now examine some double consonants with examples:

(1) When two **payir** signs combine, they do so with ***a ligature curve*** underneath, so are some others:

with phonetic value **-pp-**

(1) Same is the case with the **kay** sign, but the difference is that the shape of the hand becomes that of a **fist**:

with phonetic value **-kk-**

(2) The **caṅku** sign doubles itself:

with phonetic value **-cc-**

= **uaccan** or **uvaccan** with euphonic consonant **v**

(உவச்சன்) *'priest'*

Priest King - Google Safe Search - Labeled for reuse.

A real time inscription is:

 **1323 -11**

 = **iruccan** or **iriccan** (இருச்சன் / இரிச்சன்) *'an important rural deity sometimes called* **iriccappan** (இரிச்சப்பன்)'

Some of the real time inscriptions are:

 **1540 -11**

 **2117 -11**

 **4440 -22**

 **4657 -22**

In the 3rd inscription, 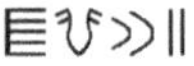 is to be read as **iriccanār** (இரிச்சனார்)'

15.06 The famous sign which redoubles itself to generate a double consonant combo is:

 +  =  **(-mm-, -nn-)**

The others are:

(1) ⋈ + ⋈ = ⋈⋈
(2) ⊥⊥⊥ + ⊥⊥⊥ = ⊥⊥⊥⊥
(3) 大 + 大 = 大大
(4) ○ + ○ = ◎
(5) ✕ + ✕ = ※
(6) ⋀⋁ + ⋀⋁ = ⋀⋁⋀⋁
(7) ⋀⋀⋀ + ⋀⋀⋀ = ⋀⋀⋀⋀⋀⋀

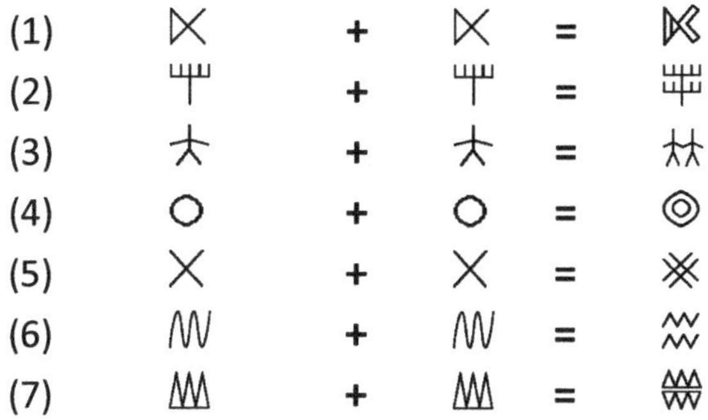

However, we aren't sure as to whether the doubled complex sign refers to some newer logogram or modified / fortified phonetic value. In the above list of 7 items, the first one has already been explained as:

⋈ **ṭ / ṟ** (ட/ற) + ⋈ **ṭ / ṟ** (ட/ற) = ⋈⋈ **ṭṭ / ṟṟ** (ட்ட/ற்ற).

We have also pointed out that the complex sign ⋈⋈ **ṭṭ / ṟṟ** has subsequently been replaced by ⋈⋈

15.07 The second item has no problem. The sign ⊥⊥⊥ has the logogram value of **peru, neṭu** (பெரு, நெடு) etc. and the phonetic value of **ya** (ய). Hence, the complex sign has the phonetic value of **yya** (ய்ய).

The third item is **not** a complex sign, but only a repeated simple sign. We already have a conventional rule that whenever a sign repeats itself, the constituent components **do not** assume the same logogram value. Such repeated signs usually denote two variant logograms.

For example, in the present case, the repeated sign should be read as **aṭi āḷ (அடியாள்)** which is not only meaningful but also a survivor-word for over 4000 years.

The fourth one is the **akam** sign we already know, namely, ○ denoting place, enclosed area etc. and the complex sign **'circle inside circle'** ◎ denotes a **well** following the Mesopotamian practice; it has the logogram value of **kiṇaṟu** (கிணறு) **kēṇi** (கேணி) and phonetic syllabic values **kiṇa** (கிண) **kē**(கே) **, kī** (கீ) . However, the sign may be named as **kēṇi** (கேணி)

In the usual course, the **kēṇi** (கேணி) sign should have yielded the phonetic syllable **ṇi** (ணி) as in the case of **ḻi** (ழி) from **kōḻi** (கோழி). However, it is not the case because there is already an identified sign for **ṇi** (ணி) derived from the **ēṇi** (ஏணி) sign **.** The sign is named as **ēṇi** (ஏணி).

◎ **= kiṇaṟu** (கிணறு) **kēṇi** (கேணி) and phonetic syllabic values **kiṇa** (கிண) **kē**(கே) **, kī** (கீ) .

 = **yēṇi** (யேணி), **ēṇi** (ஏணி) and phonetic syllabic values **ṇi** (ணி).

15.08 A close scrutiny of Indus signs reveals that several signs have two variants, one of ***normal size*** and the other of ***minuscular size***, with or without a change in shape. The following signs keep original shape in reduced size:

(1) 

○ **am** +  **pa** >>  **ampa**

akam + pai/vai >> akavai

akam + ppai >> akappai

kalam + pai/vai >> kalavai

we may name the sign as **akavai (அகவை).**

we may name the sign as **akappai (அகப்பை).**

we may name the sign as **kalavai (கலவை);**

and others which will be interpreted and named in latter pages, are:

(2)

am + ka >> aṅka

ṭ/ṟ + ka >> ṭ/ṟ ka

we may name the sign **ṭka / ṟka**

and others which will be interpreted and named in latter pages, are:

(3)

manṟu + varai >> manṟapam

/maṇṭapam *'public hall, memorial'.* ***The sign literally means mountainous or huge hall.***

we may name the sign  as **maṇṭapam (மண்டபம்).**

15.09 On the other hand, we notice also that the minuscular form, particularly in the case of **payir** and **kay** signs, occurs *twice* or sometimes *thrice* to form a complex sign.

When you look at the first two, we get a doubt as to whether the **kay** sign is added twice for its double occurrence in words or for aesthetic reasons to ensure symmetry of shape. For example, the second can be split and interpreted as follows:

 **(kay pa<u>r</u><u>r</u>u ka** *'to hold hand'* as in wedlock*)*. Or simply as

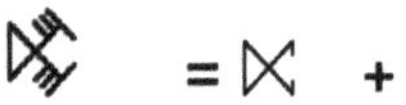 **(pa<u>r</u><u>r</u>u ka** *'to hold hand' as in wedlock) reserving the thrice occurring* ***kay*** *sign for full expression maintaining symmetry also:*

 **(kay pa<u>r</u><u>r</u>u ka** *'to hold hand' as in wedlock* **(கை பற்றுக / கை பிடிக்க).**

 is logogram for both the words **piṭi** (பிடி) 'catch' and **pa<u>r</u><u>r</u>u** (பற்று) *'hold'.*

However, for the purpose of analysis and research, we may call the sign  as **pa<u>r</u><u>r</u>uka** (பற்றுக) and the sign  as **kay-pa<u>r</u><u>r</u>uka (கை-பற்றுக)**

15.10 The mini horn or triangular shape you frequently meet on the sides of the normal signs is the minuscular form of well-known **tēn** sign,  which has the phonetic value, **ṭu** (டு).

 **maṭu (மடு)**

 **caṭu (சடு)**

 **ccaṭu (-ச்சடு)**

 **kaṇṭu (கண்டு)**

 **-ntāṭu (-ந்தாடு)**

 **ṭu (ஜயமுண்டு)**

 **ṭuṇṭu (-டுண்டு** as in கட்டுண்டு**)**

Let me try to clarify the situation by explaining with full details one particular example, say,

 **= kaṇṭu (கண்டு)**

We already know that the **akam**  sign has not only the phonetic value, **am,** but also another logographic value of **uḷ** (உள்) *'inside'.* Hence,

 **uḷ** (உள்) **+**  **ṭu** (டு) **=**  **uṇṭu** (உண்டு)

Please bear in mind that in Tamil,

uḷ + tu >> uḷ + ṭu = uṇṭu
koḷ + tu >> koḷ + ṭu = koṇṭu
kaṇ + tu >> kaṇ + ṭu = kaṇṭu

Here is an interesting example:

 **aṟam +**  **uṇṭu**  **= aṟamuṇṭu** (அறமுண்டு) *'there exists dharma'*

15.11 While interpreting the Indus Signs, it is quite profitable to assume that the circumflex sign, Λ whenever it occurs **in combos**, is an instant of **u** (உ) **sound,** *with or without* some consonant sounds like **ku, vu, yu, tu** (கு, வு, யு, து) etc.

At the same time, we should not expect minute exactness in phonetic values, *there will always be* ***nuances in sound values*** which can only be determined by the expert scribes on one hand and experienced readers on the other. For instance, the well-known **paku sign** X has phonetic values with nuances on the final vowel, such as, **paku, paka, paki:**

 **= | ra, ru, r + Λ ku, vu**

 **= | r + Λ vu >> rvu (ர்வு)**

 **= pakirvu (பகிர்வு)**

 **= paka + vu >> pakavu (பகவு)** *'share'.*

When the **paku** sign is impregnated with the **divinity** sign, we get:

 **= paka + vān >> pakavān (பகவான்)** *'celestial God'.*

Coming to some other signs with the circumflex sign, we can note the following:

 **:** There is only one inscription containing this sign. It is from Mohenjo Daro site,  **1548 -11**

The sign is a combination of more than two signs. The **iru** sign  in oblique position may be considered as the divinity determinative. Hence, the whole complex sign should refer to some **god** or **deity**.

The remaining signs in this unique inscription, namely,  is to be interpreted as the sun god, **pakalōn (பகலோன்)**, or the deity, **ellaiyan (எல்லையன்)** which reinforces our divination that the whole complex sign should refer to some god/deity.

Interestingly, a graffiti considered similar to this sign, has been discovered in the excavations in Tamil Nadu, particularly in **Porunai Civilization** area.

A similar complicated multi-pronged complex sign is the following:

Now coming to other complex signs containing the circumflex sign, we have:

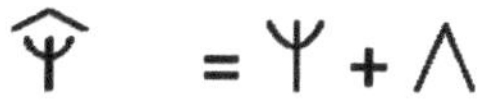 >> **puvvu** or **pū** *'flower'* ??

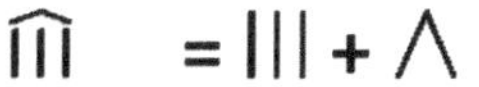 >> **mutuvu, mutuku (முதுவு, முதுகு)**

 >> **-lvu, -ṟku (-ல்வு, -ற்கு)**

Now look at the following two complex signs made up of two very well-known and frequently occurring simple signs:

Elsewhere, we have derived the guideline that whenever two simple signs of **equal size**, one above the other, combine to form a complex sign, we should read the complex sign from top to bottom *vide* ***Guideline 010***. Hence,

There is another important observation which should be studied carefully by the reader and borne in mind. While two or more simple signs combine to form a complex sign, a sign with symmetric parts splits into two and enclose the other sign or signs.

Some examples will clear this point. The oval or circle shaped sign with the phonetic value **am** ○ usually splits into two halves in the shape of **brackets, the iru** sign || with two vertical strokes splits into two single strokes, the **acca** sign)) with two curved strokes splits into two single curved stroke etc.

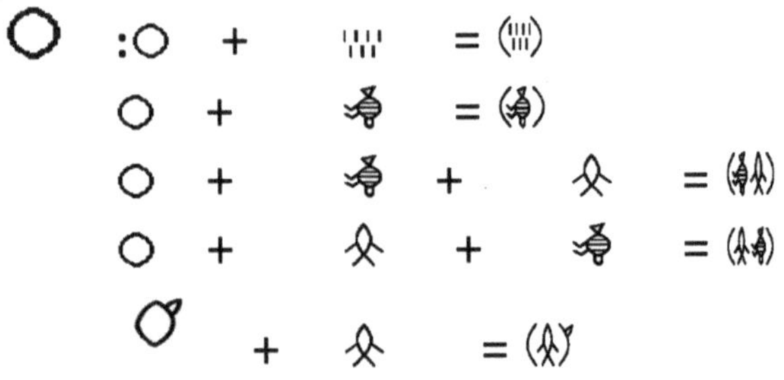

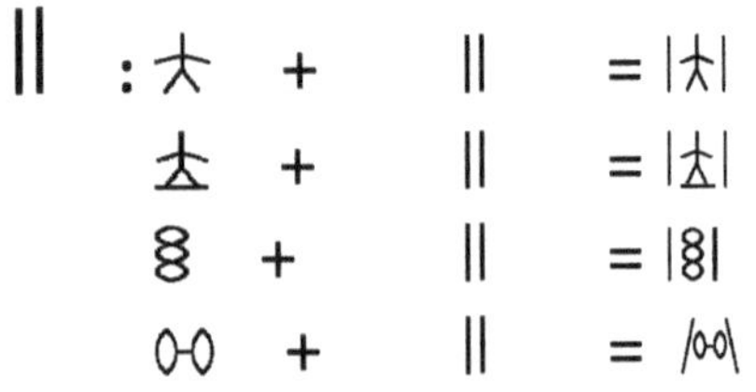

(tilting of strokes is for aesthetic purpose)

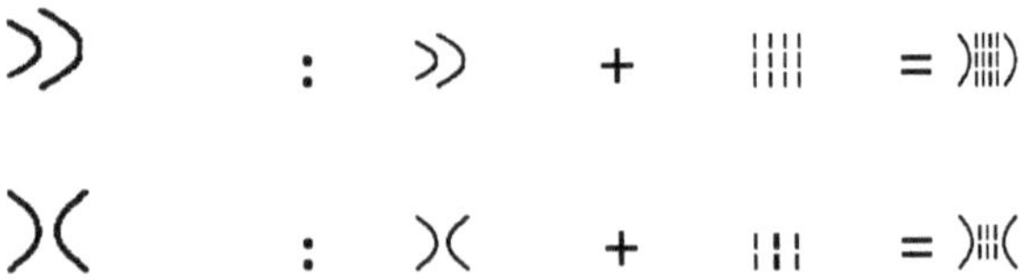

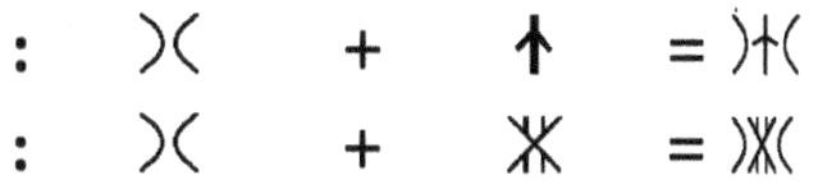

As regards the complex sign,  I have my own theory, whereas some scholars feel that it is the combination of **mān** sign,  and **iru** sign .

I feel that the **yāṟu** sign meaning ***river,***  has later been rotated 90^0 anticlockwise in order to save horizontal space as in the case of Mesopotamian cuneiform and represented as .

16. Vowel Combos

16.01 Unlike modern South Asian scripts in general and Dravidian scripts in particular, where pure vowels usually occur only initially in a word, ***the fish signs identified as vowels occur everywhere in the Indus Script.*** Hence, it is necessary that we examine various aspects involved with vowels in some detail.

While discussing about the vowel combos, let us bear in mind that the long vowel,  **ā** and the diphthong,  **ai** or **ay** are considered as ***single simple signs*** for all practical purposes.

As such the simple vowel signs in the Indus Script are the following 7:

Out of these ***seven***, the two  serve not only as ***long vowels*** (in initial position of words), but also as ***phonetic modifiers*** as already learnt in earlier chapters, and except the simple fish sign  , the others do not reduplicate. Hence, theoretically we can have 7 X 7 = 49 **two-vowel combos**. However, in actual practice, not all combinations occur.

Let us now list out all ***possible combos*** which occur and ***impossible combos*** which do not occur in the Indus script:

With  as first vowel:

(a) possible: 3

(b) impossible: 4

With  as first vowel:

(a) Possible: 2

(b) impossible: 5

With  as first vowel:

(a) **Possible: 3**

(b) impossible: 4

With  as first vowel:

(a) **Possible: 5**

(b) impossible: 2

With  as first vowel:

(a) **Possible: 6**

(b) impossible: 1

With  as first vowel:

(a) **Possible: 4**

(b) impossible: 3

With  as first vowel:

(a) **Possible: 2**

(b) impossible: 5

16.02 We have seen that in the Indus Script, pure vowel signs occur ***within words*** quite frequently. How to address this issue and find plausible and reasonable explanations.

We have already seen that **euphonic consonants** play a significant role in word building exercises in Dravidian Languages in general and Classical Tamil in particular, but in Harappan ***writing system*** euphonic consonants are **totally ignored** and did not find a place in signs. For example, the deity name **murukan** is a combination of the stem **muru** and universal upper class ending **an,** as indicated below:

muru + an >> muru + k + an

The Indus Script had, therefore, signs only for **muru** and **an** and the reader is expected to supply the euphonic consonant **k.**

 **muru +  an >>  murukan**

This practice extends to syllables containing vowels.

 **ā +  an >>  ātan**

 **ā +  i >>  āti**

 **ā +  uṭai >>  āvuṭai**

16.03 What are the frequently used prominent euphonic add-ons? We may cite the following:

v, y, t, k, n etc.

However, it is not possible to formulate any strict rules in this regard. We have to learn them only through experience.

For example, let us see how to interpret the following:

 Phonetic syllable **a**

 Phonetic syllable **i**

non-class ending **iy , i**

a + v + i >> avi

i + n + i >> ini

>> **avini** (அவினி) *female cohort of ātan'*

Please see a real-time inscription:

4604 -22

It is to be read as **aviniyār** (அவினியார்).

16.04 Among the works included in Sangam Literature, one of the oldest is **aiṅkuṟunūṟu** (ஐங்குறுநூறு).

The opening 10 poems of the anthology begin with invocation to sun-God, **ātan** and his female cohort, **avini**:

வாழி ஆதன், வாழி அவினி

(vāḻi ātan, vāḻi avini) *'Hail ātan, Hail avini'*

The reader should not get the wrong impression that the word ***ātan*** has fallen into disuse; on the contrary, as pointed out in some other place in the book, it re-appears in Tamil Brahmi or **tamiḻi** (தமிழி) Script in Keezhadi excavations.

Further, as I have frequently pointed out elsewhere in the book that several words beginning with a vowel has added a dental **ta** (த) or **na** (ந) in later period. For instance, **iru** (இரு) became **tiru** (திரு), **aṅkai** (அங்கை) became **naṅkai** (நங்கை), **ampi** (அம்பி) became **nampi** (நம்பி) etc.

In the same vein, **ātan** (ஆதன்) became **nātan** (நாதன்) as found in medieval literature. **nātan** (நாதன்) in Tamil and **nāthan / nāth** elsewhere are only dentalised version of **ātan** (ஆதன்)

17. Bi-vowel syllables

17.01 There is special type of syllabary in Tamil, which is typical and requiring some explanation. In English prosody, stresses on words play a vital role and they are of two kinds, weak stresses and strong stresses. In Tamil, the length of vowels plays important role in multi-vowel words. Compare the following pairs:

koḻi (கொழி) - **kōḻi** (கோழி)

cati (சதி) - **cāti** (சாதி)

paṭam (படம்) - **pāṭam** (பாடம்)

koṭai (கொடை) - **kōṭai** (கோடை)

kōḻi (கோழி), **cāti** (சாதி), **pāṭam** (பாடம்), **kōṭai** (கோடை) with *first vowel long*, are **two-syllabic words**.

While **koḻi** (கொழி), **cati** (சதி), **paṭam** (படம்), **koṭai** (கொடை) with *first vowel short* are considered to be mono-syllabic words of **nirai** (நிரை) type if they do not end in enunciative consonants and **niraipu** (நிரைபு) type if they end in enunciative consonants as in **cātu** (சாது), **pāṭu** (பாடு), **kōṭu** (கோடு).

It may be borne in mind that *following a long vowel*, word-final single surd with enunciative **u** and double surds with enunciative **u** are treated alike in syllabary analysis. **cātu** (சாது) - **cāttu** (சாத்து), **pāṭu** (பாடு) - **pāṭṭu** (பாட்டு), **kōṭu** (கோடு) - **kōṭṭu** (கோட்டு) are treated alike.

Words like **pāṭu** (பாடு), **kōṭu** (கோடு), **'āṟu'** (ஆறு) *'six', with enunciative **u** and* **'ēḻu'** (ஏழு) *'seven'* with full **u** are called **two-letter-single-words** (ஈரெழுத்து ஒருமொழி). They are very important in developing signs for Indus Script.

Guideline 11 The following thumb-rules are adopted in developing new signs in the Indus Script.

(1) *Whenever a* ***logogram*** *denoting a multi-syllabic word, say* **'kōḻi',** (கோழி) *'fowl',* **'kōṭṭai'** (கோட்டை) *'fort, palace', or* **two-letter-single-words** (ஈரெழுத்து ஒருமொழி) like **'āṟu'** (ஆறு) *'six',* **'ēḻu'** (ஏழு) *'seven' etc. is used as* ***phonogram,*** *that is, a* ***phonetic syllable,*** *the phonetic value assigned to the sign is usually the second or last syllable or second letter, but* ***not the first.***

In the above-cited examples, they are **'ḻi'** (ழி), **'ṭṭ'** (ட்ட), **'ṟu'** (று) **'ḻu'** (ழு), **etc**. *The reason is that such syllables cannot occur word-initially in Proto-Dravidian as well as Classical Tamil.*

(2) *In compound signs made up of two basic signs, the bigger sign should be read first. For example:*

In  the first sign to read is  and  comes next.

In  the first sign to read is  and  comes next.

N.B. *An exception to the above rule occurs sometimes; whenever the inside-sign's phonetic value* ***begins in a vowel,*** *the* <u>*inside-sign is read first.*</u>

For example, the diacritic sign with usual phonetic value **'i'** occurs in three different places, upper, middle, lower:
Each of them combines with other signs to yield compound signs

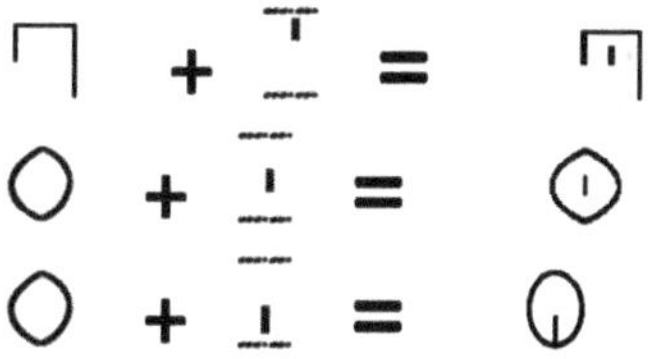

Take the third item, the usual reading is '**am + i'**, but since the inside-sign has a vowel sound it is read as **i + am**

 = **iam** (இயம்), *'statement'*

(3) ***Euphonic consonant*** *(either single or double) is introduced while combining syllables to form words, but* ***they are omitted in writing,*** *and it is left to the reader to insert them while reading written materials. For example,*

ā+i can be

*ā+y+i = ā**y**i,*

*ā+t+i = ā**t**i,*

*ā+tt+i = ā**tt**i,*

*ā+cc+i = ā**cc**i*

muru + an can be

*muru+v+an = muru**v**an,*

*muru+k+an = muru**k**an*

aru+ an can be

*aru+v+an = aru**v**an,*

*aru+k+an = aru**k**an*

iṭi + i can be

*iṭi +kk +i = iṭi**kk**i*

17.02 I have interpreted some of the signs as described hereunder:

The logogram  = akam is derived from **a + am** with the addition of 'k' which is a euphonic consonant. It is also used as per thumb-rule (1) above as phonetic syllable **'am'** where **'m'** is only a nasalizing consonant, but not proper **'m'**. This nasal sound occurs as:

ṅ before **k** as in **caṅku** சங்கு ,

ñ before **c** as in **nañcu** நஞ்சு,

ṇ before **ṭ** as in **naṇṭu** நண்டு,

n before **t** as in **pantu** பந்து,

m before **p** as in **ampu** அம்பு,

ṉ before **ṟ** as in **kaṉṟu** கன்று,

Let us now consider the logogram  = **'payir'** (பயிர்), **'nel'** (நெல்) which also serves as *phonetic syllable* **'pai / pay '** (பை / பய்).

In word-final position, the phonetic syllable has a weak indeterminate sound, **'-a'**(-அ), **'-ai'** (-ஐ), **'-i'** (-இ), **'-u'** (-உ)

 **'ampV'** where word-final **V** represents any weak short indeterminate sound, **'-a'**(-அ), **'-ai'** (-ஐ), **'-i'** (-இ), **'-u'** (-உ) However, preferred phonetic value in this example is **'ampi'** (அம்பி) with its later form **'nampi'** (நம்பி) denoting a *gentleman or male person.*

Similarly, as per my interpretation:

 = **(logographic) 'kai'** (கை), *hand, arm;* **(phonetic syllable)** 'kai / kay /ka' (கை / கய்). In word-final position, the phonetic syllable has a weak indeterminate sound, **'-a'**(-அ), **'-ai'** (-ஐ), **'-i'** (-இ), **'-u'** (-உ)

 **'aṅkV',** where word-final **V** represents any weak short indeterminate sound, **'-a'**(-அ), **'-ai'** (-ஐ), **'-i'** (-இ), **'-u'** (-உ). However, the preferred sound in the present example is **'aṅkai'** (அங்கை) with its later form **'naṅkai'** (நங்கை) denoting a *lady or female person.*

This type of compound signs have three positionally determined phonetic values.

 = **aṅk-** in word-initial position;

= **-ṅk-** in word-medial position;

= **- ṅkV** in word-final position; the final -V is a short indeterminate sound, **'-a'**(-அ), **'-ai'** (-ஐ), **'-i'** (-இ), **'-u'** (-உ).

Similarly,

 = **amp-** in word-initial position;

= **-mp-** in word-medial position;

= **-mV** in word-final position; the final -V is a short indeterminate sound, **'-a'**(-அ), **'-ai'** (-ஐ), **'-i'** (-இ), **'-u'** (-உ).

17.03 We have earlier seen that the Harappan language used in the Indus Valley grouped nouns into two classes:

(1) **uyar-tiṇai** (உயர்திணை) 'higher class' to which belonged gods, deities, male humans, etc., and

(2) **aĥṟinai** (அஃறிணை) 'non-class' to which belonged singular female humans, animals, the inanimate beings etc.

17.04 We are now living in an era of ***gender neutrality***, but it was not the case even just before a few decades. Gender neutrality is an effort to discourage the use of gender-specific professional titles such as *chairman, watchman, nurse* etc. Even gender-neutral professional titles like professor, artist, philosopher, mathematician etc. usually referred to the male; these neutral professional titles as well as the gender specific titles mentioned above required a qualifying epithet when a necessity arises to denote the female or male gender of the title holders. For example:

Chairman > lady chairman, Watchman > lady watchman, Nurse > male nurse; Midwife > male midwife, Professor > lady professor, Artist > female artist, Philosopher > woman philosopher, Mathematician > woman mathematician, etc.

17.04 In Indus language, there were universal **uyar-tiṇai** (உயர்திணை*), higher class* and **aħṟiṇai** (அஃறிணை), *lower class* word endings:

 = male specific higher class ending, usually pronounced **as -aṉ** (-அன்), sometimes *(mostly after stems ending in consonant)* **as -ōṉ** (-ஓன்)

 = female specific non-class ending, usually pronounced as **-i** (-இ), sometimes *(mostly after stems ending in vowels 'I' and 'ai')* as **-ai** (-ஐ)

When these endings are added to the stem it is usual to introduce euphonic consonant or consonants, which are confined to reading and speaking only but **not** to writing; the prominent being:

the liquid ones: **-y-** (ய்), and **-v-** (வ்)

surds: **-t-** (த்), **-tt-** (த்த்), **-k-** (க்), **-kk-** (க்க்) etc.

Further we also have:

 = **gender neutral honorific plural affix,** usually pronounced as **ār** (ஆர்); it was also used as plural particle **kaḷ** (கள்); whenever double plural as in the case of **aṭiyārkaḷ, aṭikaḷār** (அடியார்கள், அடிகளார்) is required, the double sign  is used.

17.05 Further in Tamil and Malayalam words ending in semi-nasal **-am** adds **-tt-** before taking on syllables like "in" "āl" etc.

mara(m) (tree) + il (in) >>>> mara + tt + il = marattil (in the tree). See also the Kannada case.[2]

This practice has, I think, its origin in the Harappan Language. *In a logo-syllabic script like the Indus Script, you cannot expect add-ons meant for euphonic purposes to have their own separate signs. Hence,* *no separate signs are available for such euphonic add-ons and the readers are expected to fill in the gaps, based on their knowledge.*

Whenever a syllable ending in a vowel adds another syllable beginning with the same or another vowel, invariably adds a euphonic consonant or consonants *in absentia* for reading purposes.

The most usual euphonic consonants to be added are the liquid ones, **'y'** and **'v'.**

However, the Harappan Language seems to have some sort of propensity towards **'t'** (த்) and **'tt'** (த்த) and 'n' (ண்)

This practice is not confined to the combinations of syllables to form words, but ***also to stand-alone vowel-ending syllables.***

The numeral sign ||| has, among others, phonetic syllabic value **'mu'(**மு) which is *suo motu* extended to **'mut'** and **'mutt'** with enunciative vowel **'u'**:

||| = **mu** (மு)**, mutu**(முது)**, muttu**(முத்து)

Similarly, the numeral sign '¦¦' has among others, phonetic syllabic value **'el̲u'(**எழு) which is *suo motu* extended to **'elut'** and **'ezutt'** with enunciative vowel **'u'**:

'¦¦' = **el̲u** (எழு)**, el̲utu**(எழுது)**, el̲uttu**(எழுத்து)

---

[2] The equivalent Kannada words ending in semi-liquid 'a' adds a 'd' before taking on a syllable beginning with vowel. In Dravidian languages, a surd like k, p, t, t sandwiched between two vowels becomes voiced (soft) (k > g), (p > b), (t > d), (t > d)

Mara (tree) + alli (in) >>>> mara + d + alli = maradalli (ಮರದಲ್ಲಿ) (in the tree)

18. *Some Illustrative Examples*

22.01 In this chapter, we are going to learn some interesting but illustrative examples.

Is there a chance to form any plausible interpretation to the following simple inscription in which the **kai** sign,  is repeated thrice:

 **7201-44**

In the first instance, let us bear in mind the convention followed by the Harappan Scholars as explained in a guideline:

> ***Guideline 06*** *Usually, a sign in the Indus Script has more than one logogram values and a couple of phonetic syllabic values; whenever such a sign occurs in double,* ***it is almost an unwritten law that each component of the double sign will have a different value****, never repetition of the same value. This result is applicable to triple or quadruple occurrence of a sign also.*

However, any combination of different meanings of **kai** sign,  does not seem to yield an intelligent word. The sign in question qualified by numerals usually denotes length measurement, **muḻam** (முழம்) 'cubit $1^3/_2$ foot, defined in Tamil as the length between elbow to the tip of stretched middle finger. Hence,  would usually mean 3 cubits; so if you want to express the meaning of 3 hands, what you do is to repeat the **kai** sign thrice as in the case of  meaning 3 measures as we have seen in the previous chapter while trying to interpret the first line of the longest Indus Script inscription running to three lines.

I am not still convinced. I feel that in the present situation the  might mean **third-hand** likely denoting a helper or assistant to serve the master as third hand. It makes sense in this case.

 **= mūnṟām kaiyāḷ** (மூன்றாம் கையாள்) *'Third-hand person, helper, assistant'*

18.02 The next one is an interesting example.

 1337-11

The sign  has logogram value **vāy** (வாய்) *'mouth'. And the sign*  *has the principal value of* **ural** (உரல்) *and its cogent phonetic values, particularly* **urai** (உரை). **vāyuraittal** (வாயுரைத்தல்) had the meaning of ***'praising.'***

 = **vāy** (வாய்) *'mouth'.*

 = **urai** (வாய்) *'praise'.*

 = **-ppa** (-ப்ப), *a double consonant already learnt.*

 = **takka** (தக்க), *a complex word already learnt.*

 = **aracu, āṭci** (அரசு, ஆட்சி).

▪ = **i, itu, iḫtu** (இ, இது, இஃது), *a diacritic sign already learnt.*

The whole inscription can be interpreted as shown below:

 = **vāyuraippa takka aracu itu**

(வாயுரைப்பத் தக்க அரசு இது), *this is a praiseworthy Government.*

vāyuraippa (pōṟṟa) takka āṭci iḣtu வாயுரைப்ப (போற்ற) தக்க ஆட்சி இஃது

22.03 Let us now go to the next example from Harappa:

 **4081-22**

H-25 a

A close examination of the given inscription reveals that the same can be split up into components for ease of interpretation.

We have dealt with the sign  on several occasions, and we also know that the sign is grandly multi-valued. Taking into account the next component, it is felt that the sign can have most probably either of the two values, namely, **pakal** (பகல்) 'daytime', and **pāl** (பால்), *'milk, white.'*

Elsewhere in this book, we have also opined that the best and practical interpretation to the three-sign expression,  is **udai** in the sense of **uniform.** Hence,

 = **day uniform பகல் உடை** or **white uniform வெள்ளை உடை**

 = **பெண் முசிறியன்** or **முசிறிப் பெண்**

The whole expression can now be interpreted as

 = **pakal uṭai muciri peṇ** (பகல் உடை முசிறிப் பெண்), *'white uniformed woman from Musiri.'day uniformed woman from Musiri'.*

Or

 = **pāl / veḷḷai uṭai muciri peṇ** (பால் / வெள்ளை உடை முசிறிப் பெண்), *'white uniformed woman from Musiri'.*

22.04 I have often felt that instead of choosing some Indus Script inscription or the other and trying to decipher it, why not write some sentence in classical or Modern Tamil and try to translate it into Harappan Language. Here comes one such exercise. Consider the following sentence:

aṅkāḷappanār makan murukavēl, nēṟṟu tiruvaiyāṟu iravu kadaiyil, 8 mūṭṭai kōti koṇṭān

அங்காளப்பனார் மகன் முருகவேல், நேற்று திருவையாறு இரவு-கடையில் 8 மூட்டை கோதுமை கொண்டான் (வாங்கினான்).

Please study the following explanations:

 = **aṅkāḷa** (அங்காள) *'ankaali, kaali'*

 = **aṅkāḷappan** (அங்காளப்பன்) *'name of a person'*

There are reasons to believe that the consonants **r, l** and voiced surd **ḍ** interchange in Dravidian Languages; **neru** in **nerunal** is in all probability **neḍu** or as per our conventional transliteration **neṭu;** so ***yesterday*** could have been **neṭunal** (நெடுநல்). Hence,

 = **peru, neṭu** (பெரு, நெடு) *'big, tall, long'*

 = **nal** (நல்)

 = **neṭunal** (நெடுந / நெருநல்)) *'yesterday'*

Coming to the next word in the text, we get

 = **kaṇ** (கண்) 'in'

 = **al** (அல்) 'night'

 = **aṅkāṭi** (அங்காடி) 'shop'

 = **allaṅkāṭi** (அல்லங்காடி) 'night shop'

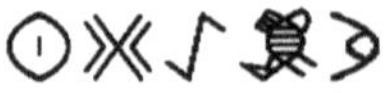 = **allaṅkāṭi kaṇ** (அல்லங்காடி கண்) 'in the night shop'

 = **eṭṭu pai / mūṭṭai** (எட்டு பை / மூட்டை) 'eight bags'

 = **kōti** (கோதி) '*wheat*

 = **koḷ + ḍu + ān** (கொள் + டு +ஆன் >> கொண்டான்) *'bought'*

The expression, **அங்காளப்பனார் மகன் முருகவேல், நேற்று திருவையாறு இரவு-கடையில் 8 மூட்டை கோதுமை கொண்டான் (*வாங்கினான்*)** can be written in the Indus Script as:

19. Long, Longer, Longest Inscriptions…

25.01 The average length of texts in the excavated Indus Inscriptions is only about **Five**. Hence, for the sake of arguments, we may consider texts with more than five signs as **long inscriptions,** texts with more than twice the average, namely **10** as **longer inscriptions.** As per the records the longest inscription consists of **26 signs.**

Here is an example of one **such longer inscription** with **10 signs** on a single line, treating the diphthong  as one sign:

 **5256 -22**

For ease of analysis, I'd like to split the text into five parts,

(1) 

(2) 

(3) 

(4) 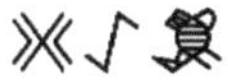

(5) 

In the Harappan Language, the ending vowel in multi-syllabic words is always *indeterminate*; so is the case with  which can pronounced as **aṅka, aṅki, aṅku, aṅkai** and to make it determinate with intended sound, we add a *phonetic indicator.* In the present case,  *used as phonetic indicator tells the reader that the final sound value is* ***ai****. Hence,*

 = **aṅkai** (அங்கை) later on **naṅkai** (நங்கை) 'lady'

The second part  is susceptible to **two** interpretations as you can see. The sign  has been interpreted as **seat (aṇai - அணை), to sit (amar - அமர்).** The end sound in **aṇai – அணை** also occurs as **i** giving an alternative interpretation of  as aṇi (அணி) meaning among others **jewel.**

Coming to the third part, please recollect what we have explained in **<u>Guideline 11</u>** as extracted below:

> *For example, the sign  was created through motivation from the shape of crescent moon. It is a multi-valued sign with values, **al** (night-time), **irā** (night), **mati** (moonlight), **intu** (moon), **iruḷ** (darkness) etc. However, there are reasons to believe that the sign was originally created to cater to the generic Harappan word for moon, **intu.** Hence, **intu** is the <u>principal value</u> or <u>default value</u> of the sign. Phonetic syllabic value of the sign **nta** (ந்த) was derived from this sense only.*

Hence, one interpretation to the pair of signs  is **aṇainta** (அணைந்த) 'belonging / pertaining to' and the first three parts of the text under examination,  is **aṅkai aṇainta** (அங்கை அணைந்த) *'pertaining to ladies'.*

Another interpretation to the first two parts of the text,  *is* **aṅkai aṇi** (அங்கை அணி) *'ladies jewel'*. Leaving the third part to be interpreted as **al** (அல்) *'night'.*

The fourth part of the text, 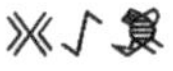 is well-known expression for **aṅkāṭi** (அங்காடி) *'shop'* and the fifth and last part of the text under examination,  the word for **VIP** has also been found used to denote **owner** or **proprietor.**

Therefore, the whole inscription can be interpreted as indicated below:

 = **aṅkai aṇi al-aṅkāṭi mutalāḷi** (அங்கை அணி அல்லங்காடி முதலாளி) *'ladies jewel night-shop owner'*

OR

 = **aṅkai aṇainta aṅkāṭi mutalāḷi** (அங்கை அணைந்த அங்காடி முதலாளி) *'ladies special shop owner'*

25.02 The following is the longest inscription in the Indus Script so far unearthed. Please remember, I have promised in the Teaser that ***the reader himself is going to interpret this longest inscription*** under my guidance:

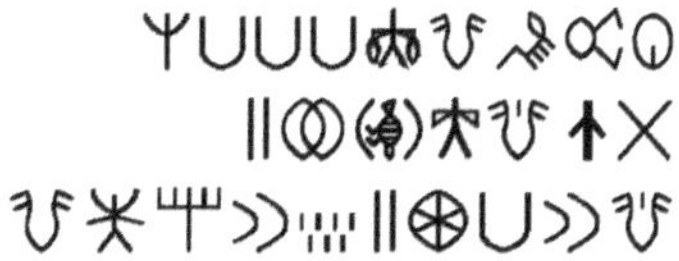

As per the documentation by Iravatham Mahadevan (Mahadevan, Indus Script : Texts, Concordance and Tables 1977), there are two instances of this Longest Inscriptions, both found in Mohenjo Daro as extracted below purely for scientific and research purposes:

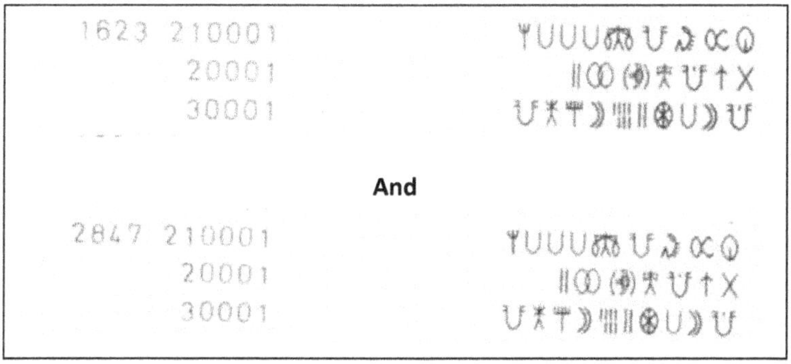

In my opinion based on analytic research, the sign occurring in the initial position of the *third line* should be the last sign in the second line only, this is a problem arising out of splitting the text during inscribing. The three **revised** lines are:

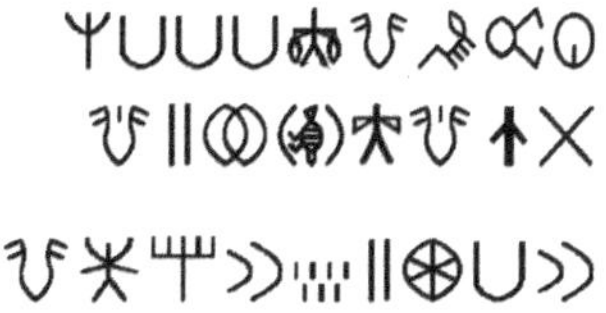

25.03 It is a known fact that the South Indians in general and Tamils in particular have been using the word **aṟam** not only in the sense of *dharma,* but also in the sense of *'gift, endowment'. A few years back, whenever you happened to visit a temple, big or small, you could not fail to notice that apart from some rectangular or square placards of various sizes fixed to the walls, depicting full details of donors, every single electric lamp, whether it is was a bulb or a tube light carried some writings; those writings were info on the donors; they were sometimes so large that they even blocked the light emanating from the lamps. The legend in such writings is titled* ***upayam*** (உபயம்).

That ***upayam*** (உபயம்) is **aram** (அறம்) if you do it once. In case if you make it permanent with a schedule for execution, then it is called an endowment **aṟakaṭṭaḷai** (அறக்கட்டளை), where the word **kaṭṭaḷai** means *'order, command.'*

We have seen that this concept is pictured by a plain fish sign in the Indus Script.

 = **aram (அறம்),** and phonetic syllable short **'a'.**

We have earlier pointed out that the Harappans used this plain fish sign **also** in the sense of **gift / donation** (உபயம் / தருமம்) and that there are about 16 inscriptions containing the fish sign as solo with the meaning of gift / donation, like the following specimen:

 **2133 -11 -1**
 **4437 -22 -3**
 **8052 -55 -16**

A overwhelming majority of inscriptions discovered in Tamil Nadu on different media pertain to donations / endowments made by royalties as well as other affluent persons to temples and for other public service schemes such as digging wells, desilting lakes, constructing and maintaining ***inns*** (choultries[3]) for travellers etc.

[3] Choultry is **a resting place, an inn or caravansary for travelers, pilgrims or visitors to a site,** typically linked to Buddhist, Jain and Hindu temples. They are also referred to as chottry, choultree, chathra, choltry,

25.04 There is a fat chance that the word for endowment was in those days **iam** (இயம்), which has become **kaṭṭaḷai** (கட்டளை) later on. **iam** (இயம்) is a substantive derived from the verb **iambu** (இயம்பு) meaning *'assert, declare, state loudly and authoritatively'.*

*The **Guideline 21** already learnt is **partly** extracted below:*

> *. . . In compound signs made up of two basic signs, the bigger sign should be read first. For example:*
>
> **In** = ○ + the first sign to read is ○ and comes next.
>
> **In** = ○ + the first sign to read is ○ and comes next.
>
> ***N.B.*** *An exception to the above rule occurs sometimes; whenever the inside-sign's phonetic value **begins in a vowel**, the* *inside-sign is read first.*

○ **am** (அம்) + **kāḷ** (காள்) ***'black, crow'*** **=** **aṅkāḷ** (அங்காள்) ***'goddess',*** because the inside sign begins with a consonant sound.

○ **am** (அம்) **+** **ē<u>l</u>** (ஏழ்) **=** **ē<u>l</u>am** (ஏழம்) ***but not*** **amē<u>l</u>** (அமேழ்), because the inside sign begins with a vowel sound.

The only numeral sign that occurs inside the brackets of **am** sign is seven **7 e<u>l</u>u, ē<u>l</u>u, ē<u>l</u>** (எழு, ஏழு, ஏழ்). Do you understand what is meant by **ē<u>l</u>am** (ஏழம்)**?** It is an ancient country adjusting Sumeria. It is in present day Iran while Sumeria is in present day Iraq.

---

chowry, chawari, chawadi, choutry, chowree or tschultri. This term is more common in South India...(Wikipedia)

 = **ē<u>l</u>am** (ஏழம்), ***'Elam'***

There are in all more than 21 inscriptions containing the text, . Please see below a few samples from different regions:

1231 -11 -1
4344 -22
7203 -44
9102 -66

25.05 Coming now to the modified second line ***viz.***
 we are acquainted with all the signs occurring therein. *Let us examine them one by one.*

X = **paku, paka** (பகு, பக) *'Divide, distribute, apportion'*. In the present instance, **paka** (பக) seems to be more appropriate.

↑ = **-rvu, -rku** (-ர்வு, ர்கு), phonetic syllable; a combination of two basic signs, | Λ

We should analyse more the complex sign ↑ which is made up of (**one**-stroke) | + (**koṭu**-stroke) Λ = ↑

We have already spoken a lot about the (**one**-stroke) | and the phonetic value I intend to give to the sign is:

↑ = **-rku** (ர்கு)

In so far as the Dravidian Languages in general or Tamil in particular are concerned, the suffixes **-rvu, -rku** (-ர்வு, ர்கு) commute as variants. There are hundreds of cases such as:

mataku – matavu (மதகு – மதவு),

pir̲aku – pir̲avu (பிறகு – பிறவு),

murukan – muruvan (முருவன் – முருகன்),

kal̲uku - kal̲uvu (கழுகு – கழுவு),

pal̲aku - pal̲avu (பழகு – பழவு)

I think it is a valid proposition to say that such of those words which end in **-rvu** nowadays, occurred with the ending - **rku** during the Indus Civilization.

 = ர்கு / ர்வு

 = **in** (இன்), phonetic syllable *denoting the genitive postposition.*

 = **cumai** (சுமை), *'load, burden'*, **por̲uppu** (பொறுப்பு) *'responsibility'*; *here, the latter meaning is more appropriate.*

Let us see what Tamil Lexicon says:

> **பொறுப்பு** por̲uppu , n. பொறு-. 1. Stress, pressure, burden; பாரம். 2. Prop, support, stay; முட்டு. (W.) 3. Duty, responsibility; உத்தர வாதம். 4. Importance; முக்கியம். 5. Weight of character; தகுதி. 6. Patience, forbearance; பொறுமை....

Hence,

 = **por̲uppu (பொறுப்பு)** ***'duty, responsibility'***

Reading together the above 4 signs,

 = **pakirvin por̲uppu** (பகிர்வின் பொறுப்பு) *'the responsibility to distribute'*

 = **ankāḷ** (அங்காள்) *'a Goddess'*

 = **ammai** (அம்மை) *'mother'*

 = **divinity determinative**

 = **in** (இன்), phonetic syllable *denoting the genitive postposition.*

Reading together the above 4 signs we get:

 = **ankāḷammaiyin** (அங்காளம்மையின்) *' of goddess Ankalammai'*

25.05 Let us now go to the modified third line:

We have already studied several signs representing double consonants, and one prominent among them is  which is interpreted as -**cc**- (-ச்ச்-) with phonetic value depending on its position in a word:

(Word initial)  = **acc-** (அச்ச்-)

(Word middle)  = **-cc-** (-ச்ச்-)

(Word final)  = **=cca, -cci, -ccu, -ccai** (-ச்ச, -ச்சி, -ச்சு, -ச்சை)

Let us see some real time inscriptions:

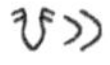 **2606 -11**

 **2117-11**

 **2122-11**

In case of solus? It is itself word initial and word final; hence

 = **accu** (அச்சு) *'print'* from which we get,

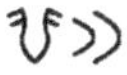 = **accan** (அச்சன்) *'printer'.*

On several occasions throughout this book, we have seen that some of the words which began in a vowel during Harappan period, have become dentalised with the addition of dental consonant like **t** (**iru** இரு >> **titu** திரு) or an **n** (**ambi** அம்பி >> **nambi** நம்பி).

Hence, in my opinion, **accan 'அச்சன்'** meaning a *printer* became **taccan** *carpenter* in later period. It is equivalent to the famous **scribe 'எழுத்தன்'** in Egypt and Mesopotamia.

Sumerian scribe:

dubsar 

Egyptian scribe:

s š 

Indus Valley scribe:

'accan' அச்சன் 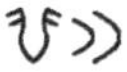

On examining the inscriptions, we find that the ***scribes*** enjoyed a very high social status in the Indus Civilization as in the case of Egyptian and Mesopotamian Civilizations. If fact, some of the scribes even scaled the social echelon to the highest level of kings or rulers.

Further, there are ample evidence to believe that the scribes in the Indus Civilization lived as a ***separate community.***

As we already know the **kalam** sign U **'கலம்'** meaning among others **tumbler** is automatically extended to denote the cogent abstract concept **kuṭi** (குடி) *'drink'. The word* **kuṭi** (குடி) has a homonym **kuṭi** (குடி) (குலம்) meaning a social class. By judicious application of Rebus Principle, the content of the sign is further extended to this social class also. Hence, I read U>> as **acca kuṭi** (அச்சக்குடி).

U>> = **acca kuṭi (**அச்சக் குடி) *'the class of scribes'*

I have my own doubt as to whether this social class still exists to this day. There is an historical account which says that the town, Karur in western Tamil Nadu was for some time the capital of Chera Kingdom and a social class called **eḻuttaccan** (எழுத்தச்சன்) originated in this area and moved west towards Kerala. There seems to be a sizable population belonging to this class and they have even a separate matrimonial website exclusively for the members of the community as learnt from Google.

We have earlier seen that the Malayalam Language, after its formation during the post-Harappan *Dravidian Languages Formative Period* from 1500 BCE to 500 BCE shared, however, the Literary Tradition with Tamil for considerably a long time, in fact, till a few centuries back.

Thunchaththu Ramanujan **Ezhuthachan,** the forerunner of Modern Malayalam is known as the Father of Malayalam language and literature. **'Ezhuthachan'** in his name may in all probability denote the class name **eḻuttaccan** (எழுத்தச்சன்).

The well-known sign ⊛ denoting usually **'āṭci'**(ஆட்சி), *rule;* **'aracu'**(அரசு), *government;* **'māṭci'** (மாட்சி), *governance,* adds the divinity determinative || to mean

||⊛ = **'vēntu'** (வேந்து) *king.*

In the inscription under consideration, we may adopt this interpretation.

<u>Guideline 18</u> *The phonetic value of any sign* ***ending in a vowel*** *sound is automatically extendable to cover the cases of the sign* ***plus*** *the unrepresented suffixes,* **tu** (து) *and* **ttu** (த்து)

After a lot of discussions, we have concluded that the sign  is to be read as **e<u>l</u>u, e<u>l</u>utu, e<u>l</u>uttu** (எழு, எழுது, எழுத்து). In so far as the present inscription is concerned, **e<u>l</u>u, e<u>l</u>uttu** (எழு, எழுத்து) is more appropriate.

Word final  = **-cca (-ச்ச), -cci (-ச்சி), ccu (-ச்சு), -ccai (-ச்சை)** and the combo is to be read either as

 = **e<u>l</u>ucci** (எழுச்சி) or **e<u>l</u>uttacca** (எழுத்தச்ச),

Te next triplet is well-known:

 = **perumān** (பெருமான்), *'king, chieftain'*

Let us now try to interpret the whole third line:

 = **acca kuṭi vēntu e<u>l</u>ucca perumān (அச்சக்குடி வேந்து எழுச்சிப் பெருமான்)** *'The uprising king from* **accan** *clan'*

Or

 = **acca kuṭi vēntu e<u>l</u>uttacca perumān (அச்சக்குடி வேந்து எழுச்சிப் பெருமான்)** *'King Ezhuttachan from* ***accan*** *clan'*

Let us now go ahead to interpret the three lines contained in the whole inscription.

This is an endowment made to **Arukkan** (later on **Siva** after Vedic Period) Temple. The standing instruction is that for every harvest, three measures of paddy should go to the temple. Paddy may refer to rice, wheat or parley, as the case may be. **Kalam** measure is approximately 64.25 litres, and 3 measures will be 192.75 litres.

Everything is alright, but where does **Ankalammai** come? In South India in general and Tamil Nadu in particular, every family has its own guardian deity and it called **kula sāmi or kula deivam,** usually some kind of **aiyanār** 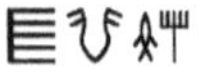 or some kind of **aṅkāḷamman** 

I think it was the practice in Indus Valley to invoke one's **family kula sāmi or kula deivam** for blessing, while making some endowments for public interest and **aṅkāḷammai**  (அங்காளம்மை) **was our**  **king's kula sāmi.**

Even today, **aṅkāḷammai**  (அங்காளம்மை) **happens to be the family kula sāmi or kula deivam** for a considerably large number of families in Tamil Nadu. In fact, the **aṅkāḷammain**  அங்காளம்மன் **at** Madagadipet in the border of Pondicherry Union Territory is the family kula sāmi or kula deivam of this book's author.

We should read the expression **aṅkāḷammaiyin** (அங்காளம்மையின்)  as **aṅkāḷammai aruḷ peṟṟa** (அங்காளம்மை அருள்பெற்ற) ***'with the grace of ankalammai.'*** Hence, the whole inscription

iyam: nal arukkan māṭṭu, mūnṟu kalam nel

pakirvin poṟuppu, aṅkāḷammaiyin

acca kuṭi vēntu eḻucca (eḻuttacca) perumān

இயம்: நல் அருக்கன் மாட்டு, மூன்று கலம் நெல்

பகிர்வின் பொறுப்பு, அங்காளம்மையின்

அச்சக்குடி வேந்து எழுச்சி (எழுத்தச்ச) பெருமான்

Statement: three measures of paddy for benevolent **Arukkan;**

Responsibility of distribution rests with Graceful **Ankalammai's**

Uprising (Ezhuttachan) King from **accan** ***clan.***

In Today's Tamil:

அறக்கட்டளை: நலஞ்செய் அருக்கனுக்கு மூன்று கலம் நெல் செலுத்த, அங்காளம்மன் அருள்பெற்ற, அச்சக்குடி வேந்தன் எழுச்சிப் (எழுத்தச்சப்) பெருமான் பொறுப்பாவார்.

End of Episode I; let's meet again in Episode II.

...*Glossary of Harappan Signs*

(1) ā (ஆ) 

(2) aincu (ஐஞ்சு)

(3) aivar (ஐவர்) 

(4) akam$_1$ (அகம்$_1$) 

(5) akam$_2$ (அகம்$_2$) 

(6) akapa (அகவை) 

(7) akappai (அகப்பை) 

(8) āḷ (ஆள்) 

(9) aḷa (அள) 

(10) āḷi (ஆளி) 

(11) amma (அம்ம) 

(12) ammaiyar (அம்மையர்) 

(13) ampiyar (அம்பியர்) 

(14) an (அன்) 

(15) ān (ஆன்) 

(16) aṅkayar (அங்கையர்) 

(17) āṇṭai *(ஆண்டை)* 

(18) antaṇar (அந்தணர்) 

(19) ār (ஆர்) 

(20) aracu (அரசு) 

(21) araiyar (அரையர்) 

(22) aṟam (அறம்) 

(23) aṟavar (அறவர்) 

(24) āṟu$_1$ (ஆறு$_1$) 

(25) āṟu$_2$ (ஆறு$_2$) 

(26) arukka (அருக்க) 

(27) aruvā (அருவா) 

(28) āṭṭi, (ஆட்டி) 

(29) avar (அவர்) 

(30) ay (ஐ) 

(31) āyar (ஆயர்) 

(32) caṅku (சங்கு) 

(33) caṭu (சடு) 

(34) cc (ச்ச) 

(35) el (எல்) 

(36) ēḻu (ஏழு) 

(37) ēṇi (ஏணி) 

(38) ēṟu (ஏறு) 

(39) ēṟuvar (ஏறுவர்) 

(40) ēvar (ஏவர்) 

(41) iam (இயம்) 

(42) ilai (இலை) 

(43) illaṟavar (இல்லறவர்) 

(44) in (இன்) 

(45) intu (இந்து) 

(46) irai (இறை) 

(47) iṟaivar (இறைவர்) 

(48) iru (இரு) 

(49) iruvar (இருவர்) 

(50) ivar (இவர்) 

(51) iy (இய்) 

(52) kā (கா) 

(53) kākkay (**காக்கை**) 

(54) kalam (கலம்) 

(55) kalappai (கலவை) 

(56) kaṇ (கண்) 

(57) kaṭavul (கடவுள்) 

(58) kāvalar (காவலர்) 

(59) kay (கை) 

(60) kāyar (*காயர்*) 

(61) kay-paṟṟuka (கை-பற்றுக) 

(62) kēṇi (கேணி) 

(63) kil̲anku (கிழங்கு) 

(64) kk (க்க) 

(65) kō$_1$ (கோ$_1$) 

(66) kō$_2$ (கோ$_2$) 

(67) koḷ (கொள்) 

(68) kōl (கோல்) 

(69) kōl̲i (**கோழி**) 

(70) kōṭṭai (கோட்டை) 

(71) koṭu (கொடு) 

(72) kōṭu (கோடு) 

(73) kōvaṇam (கோவணம்) 

(74) kūṭam (கூடம்) 

(75) kūṭu (கூடு) 

(76) ḷi (ளி) 

(77) lk or ṟk (ற்க) 

(78) ll (ல்ல) 

(79) ḷḷ (ள்ள) 

(80) mal̲ai (மழை) 

(81) mān (மான்) 

(82) maṇṭapam (மண்டபம்) 

(83) māru (மாறு) 

(84) māṭam (மாடம்) 

(85) māṭṭu *(மாட்டு)* 

(86) maṭu (மடு) 

(87) mīn (மீன்) 

(88) mītu-poli (மீது-பொலி) 

(89) mm (ம்ம) 

(90) mp (ம்ப) 

(91) mu (மு) 

(92) muni (முனி) 

(93) murukar (முருகர்) 

(94) mutu (முது)[4] 

(95) nakar (நகர்) 

(96) nāñcil (நாஞ்சில்) 

(97) naṇṭu (நண்டு) 

(98) naṭu (நடு) 

(99) naṭukaḷ (நடுகல்) 

(100) ṅk (ங்க்) 

(101) nn (ன்ன) 

(102) ṉṟ (ன்ற்) 

(103) ṇṭ (ண்ட்) 

---

[4] Explanation for calling the sign as **mutu** is available in subsequent chapters.

(104) ō (ஓது) 

(105) onpān ஒன்பான் 

(106) oru (ஒரு) 

(107) ōtuvar (ஓதுவர்) 

(108) ōvar (ஓவர்) 

(109) pakavān (பகவான்) 

(110) pakavu (பகவு) 

(111) paku (பகு) 

(112) pāṇ (பாண்) 

(113) paṟṟu$_1$ (பற்று$_1$) 

(114) paṟṟu$_2$ (பற்று$_2$) 

(115) paṟṟuka (பற்றுக) 

(116) paṭaiyal$_1$ (படையல்$_1$) 

(117) paṭaiyal$_2$ (படையல்$_2$) 

(118) paṭṭi (பட்டி) 

(119) paṭuvai (படுவை) 

(120) pay (பை) 

(121) peṟu (பெறு) 

(122) peru (பெரு) 

(123) poṟai (பொறை) 

(124) poṟaiyan (பொறையன்) 

(125) potiyam (பொதியம்) 

(126) pp (ப்ப) 

(127) ppā (ப்பா) 

(128) pū (பூ) 

(129) puṟam (புறம்) 

(130) ri (ரி) 

(131) ṟkay (ன்ற்) 

(132) ṟku (ன்ற்) 

(133) ṟp 

(134) ṟpaṭu 

(135) ṟṟ$_1$ (ற்ற$_1$) 

(136) ṟṟ$_2$ (ற்ற$_2$) 

(137) su (ஸு) 

(138) tappu (தப்பு) 

(139) taṟi (தறி) 

(140) tēn (தேன்) 

(141) ṭka / ṟka (ட்க / ற்க) 

(142) tō (தோ) 

(143) tompai (தொம்பை) 

(144) toṭu (தொடு) 

(145) toṭuvān (தொடுவான்) 

(146) tt(த்த) 

(147) tuṇaivar (துணைவர்) 

(148) tuṟai (துறை) 

(149) udaivar (உடைவர்) 

(150) ulam (உலம்) 

(151) ūṇ (ஊண்) 

(152) ural (உரல்) 

(153) uṭai (உடை) 

(154) uyar (உயர்) 

(155) vāḻ (வாழ்) 

(156) vaḷḷal (வள்ளல்) 

(157) vaṇikar (வணிகர்) 

(158) vānku (வாங்கு) 

(159) varai (வரை) 

(160) vāy (வாய்) 

(161) vēl (வேல்) 

(162) veḷar (வேளர்) 

(163) veṟiyāṭu (வெறியாடு) 

(164) vī / vē (வீ / வே) 

(165) villampu (வில்லம்பு) 

(166) vīṭu (வீடு) 

(167) vv (வ்வ) 

(168) yāḻ (யாழ்)  1

(169) yy (ய்ய) 

. . . Glossary of Harappan Words

(1)  **āṇṭavar** (*ஆண்டவர்*)

(2)  **ā** (**ஆ**, *மாடு, செல்வம்*) *'cow, cattle, wealth';*

(3)  **a** (அ); *'a'* short vowel; ph. Syl.

(4)  **ā** (ஆ); *'ā'* long vowel; ph. Syl.

(5)  **ai** (ஐ); *'elder', 'leader', 'father'*

(6)  **ai** (ஐ); an adjective for 5.

(7)  **ai / ay** (ஐ /அய்); *'ai / ay'*
diphthong; ph. Syl.

(8)  **ai āṟu** (ஐ ஆறு) *five rivers'*

(9) 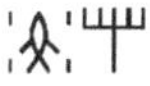 **aivar** (ஐவர்) / **aiyar** (ஐயர்)

(10)  **aivarai** (ஐ அரை / தலை நகர்)
'capital city'

(11)  **aivarai paṭṭaṇam** (ஐவரைப்
பட்டணம்) *'capital metro city'*

(12)  **aivarai paṭṭinam**
(ஐவரைப் பட்டினம்) *'Coastal Metro
city'*

(13) 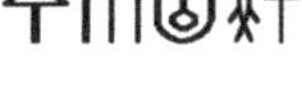 **aivaraiyam** (ஐ அரையம் /
தலை நகரம்) *'capital city-state'*

(14)  **aiyai** (ஐயை), a female Goddess

(15)  **aiyan (**ஐயன்) *'elder, leader, father'*

(16)  **aiyanār (**ஐயனார்), *'village guardian deity'*

(17)  **aiyāṟappan** (ஐயாறப்பன்), *'city guardian deity'*

(18)  **āl** (ஆள்) ***'****person'*

(19)  **āḷi (**ஆளி**)** *'Governor'* -  **āḷiy (**ஆளிய்**)** *'Governor'*

(20)  **am / tu** (அம் / து) for other non-class words

(21)  **amiḻ** (அமிழ்) *'nectar'*

(22)  **amma** (அம்ம)

(23) 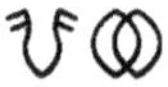 **amman** (அம்மன்) *'Mother God'*

(24)  **amman** (அம்மன்) *'Mother God'*

(25)  **amman** (அம்மன்) *'Mother God'*

(26)  **an** (அன்)

(27)  **ān** (ஆன்); Ph.Syl.

(28)  **aṇam** (அணம்) / **ṇam** (ணம்); Ph. Syl.

(29)  **aṇam** (அணம்) or **anam** (அனம்); ph.Syl.

(30)  **anam** (அனம்) / **nam** (னம்)

(31)  **ancal** (அஞ்சல்) *'announcement / messenge / news'*

(32)  **ancan** (அஞ்சன்) *'announcer / messenger / newsman'*

(33)  **añcan** (அஞ்சன்) *'messenger'*

(34)  **anka nātan** (அங்க நாடன்), *'ruler / inhabitant of Anga country'*

(35)  **ankāṭi** (அங்காடி) *'shop, market'*

(36)  **ankāṭian** (அங்காடியன்) *'shopman'*

(37)  **āṇṭai** (ஆண்டை) *'Lord'*

(38)  **āṇṭavan** (ஆண்டவன்) *'god'*

(39)  **antaṇar** (அந்தணர்)

(40)  **ār** (ஆர்); honorific plural particle

(41)  **aracāṭci** (அரசாட்சி) *'government rule'*

(42)  **arai** (அரை)

(43)  **arai** (அரை) *'to grind'*

(44)  **arai** (அரை) *'to grind'*

(45)  **aṟai** (அறை) *'chamber, cell, room'*

(46)  **araicu** (அரைசு) / **aracu** (அரசு) *'government'*

(47)  **araiyam** ***'city state'***

(48)  **araiyam** ***'city state'***

(49)  **araiyar** (அரையர்) or **aracar** (அரசர்)

(50)  ***araiyar*** (அரையர்)

(51)  **aṟam** (அறம்) *'dharma'*

(52)  **aṟamuṇṭu** (அறமுண்டு) *'there exists dharma'.*

(53)  **arappā** (அரப்பா) *'Harappa'*

(54) 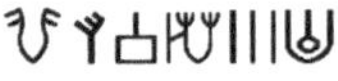 **arappā takaiyan (அரப்பா தகையன்)** *'Harappan Aristocrat'*

(55) 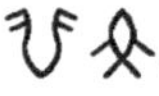 **aṟavan** (அறவன்) *'God, sage, ascetic'*

(56)  **aravar** (அறவர்) *'persons who observe* **dharma***'*

(57)  **aṟavi** (அறவி) *'Goddess, female ascetic'*

(58)  **aru** (அரு); Ph. Syl.

(59)  **āṟu** (ஆறு) *'six'*

(60)  **āṟu** (ஆறு) *'six'*

(61)  ***arukka*** *(அருக்க) /* ***arukkan*** *(அருக்கன்); name of Sun God*

(62)  **arukkan aruḷ** (அருக்கன் அருள்) *'the Grace of Arukkan'*

(63)  **arukkan māṭṭu mūṉṟu kalam₂ nel** *(அருக்கன் மாட்டு மூன்று கலம் நெல்)* 'three measures of paddy to Arukkan'

(64) 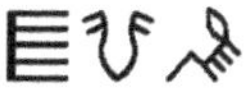 **arukkanār** (அருக்கனார்)

(65)  **aruḷ** (அருள்); Ph. Syl.

(66)  **aruḷmiku arukkan** (அருள்மிகு அருக்கன்) *'Graceful Arukkan'*

(67)  **arum** (அரும்); Ph. Syl.

(68) ___**aruvā** (அருவா); Ph. Syl.

(69)  **ātan (**ஆதன்), *'father god'*

(70)  **āṭci** (ஆட்சி) *'rule'*

 **aṭi āḷ (**அடியாள்**)** *'handyman'*

(71)  **āti, āyi, ātti, ācci** (ஆதி, ஆயி, ஆத்தி, ஆச்சி*);* ***'mother or mother God'***

(72)  **aṭiyārkaḷ / aṭikaḷār** (அடியார்கள் / அடிகளார்)

(73)  **āṭṭi,** (ஆட்டி) *'woman'*

(74)  **āṭṭu** (ஆட்டு)

(75)  **āṭṭu** (ஆட்டு) *'mill oil in oil-press' 'grate'*

(76)  **āvūr** (ஆவூர்); name of a place

(77)  **āvuṭaiyan** (ஆவுடையன்);

richman'

(78)  **āyar** (ஆயர்) / **āvar** (ஆவர்)

(79)  **caṅku (சங்கு)** ***'conch'***

(80)  **cari (**சரி) *'right / correct'*

(81)  **cekku** (செக்கு) *oil-press'*

(82)  **ciri (**சிறி) ***'sabre'***

(83)  **cuma** *(சும)*; *'be burdened', 'carry a burden'*

(84)  **e** (எ); *'e'* short vowel; ph. Syl.

(85)  **ē** (ஏ); *'ē'* long vowel; ph. Syl.

(86)  **ē** *long vowel;* ph. Syl.

(87)  **el** (எல்) / **en<u>r</u>u** (என்று) *'sun'*

(88)  **el** (எல்) ***'sun'***

(89)  **ellai** (எல்லை) *'limit / boundary'*

(90)  **ellan** (எல்லன்) **/ pakalōn***)* (பகலோன்) *'Sun-God'*

(91)  **ellappanār** (எல்லப்பனார்) *'Sun God'*

(92)  **e<u>l</u>u** (எழு), **e<u>l</u>utu**(எழுது), **e<u>l</u>uttu**(எழுத்து)

(93)  **ē<u>l</u>u** (ஏழு) 'seven'

(94)  **ēṟu** (ஏறு) *'bull, buffalo'*

(95)  **i** (இ); *'i'* short vowel; ph. Syl.

(96)  **ī** *long vowel;* ph. Syl.

(97)  **i, iy , yi, ai** (இ, இய், யி, ஐ) for non-class female human words

(98)  **iam** (இயம்), *'statement'*

(99)  **il** (இல்) *'in'* locative grammatical particle

(100)  **illaṟavar / illaṟattār** (இல்லறவர், இல்லறத்தார்) 'observer of dharma from home'

(101)  **in** (இன்); Ph.Syl.

(102)  **īr** (ஈர்) / **īram** (ஈரம்) *'water'*

(103)  **iṟai** (இறை) *'god, king'*

(104)  **iraivan (இறைவன்)**

(105) 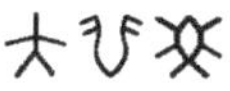 **iraivan aṭi (இறைவன் அடி)** *'servant to god / king'*

(106)  **iṟaivi** (இறைவி), *'Queen, Goddess'*

(107)  **iṟaiyūr** (இறையூர்); name of a place

(108)  **eṟaiyūr** (எறையூர்); name of a place

(109)  **iranṭām kuṭi$_2$** (இரண்டாம் குடி)

(110)  **iranṭu** (இரண்டு) / **iru** (இரு) *'two'*

(111) 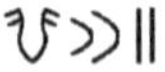 **iruccan / iriccan** (இருச்சன் / இரிச்சன்) *'an important rural deity'*

(112) 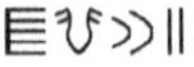 **iriccanār** (இரிச்சனார்) *'rural deity'*

(113)  **iru** (இரு) *'two'*

(114)  **iruḷ** (இருள்) *'darkness'*

(115)  **irunkō** (இருங்கோ) *'great king'*

(116)  **irunkō** (இருங்கோ) *'great king'*

(117)  **iṭai** (இடை) / **viṭai** (விடை) *'bull'*

(118)  **iṭai mīnam** (இடை மீனம்)

*"zodiac sign **taurus**"*

(119)  **iṭi** (இடி)

(120)  **iṭi** (இடி) *'to crush'*

i. ka (க)

(121)  **kā** (கா)

(122)  **ka, kay, kākka** (க, கை, காக்க); Ph.Syl.

(123)  **kākkay** (காக்கை) *'crow'*

(124)  **kal** (கல்) *'stone, 'rock'*

(125)  **kaḷ** (கள்); plural suffix

(126)  **kalam** (கலம்) *'mortar'*

(127)  **kalam (கலம்)** *'vessel, tumbler'*

(128)  **kalam** (கலம்) 'vessel, cup, basket, mortar'

(129) **kaḻi** (கழி) *'pole, mast, stick, rod, sceptre'*

(130) **kampam** (கம்பம்) *'pole, mast, stick, rod, sceptre'*

(131)  **kaṇ** (கண்) *'in'* archaic locative grammatical particle

(132)  **kār /kāḷ / karu / kari** (கார், காள், கரு/கரி) *'black'*

(133)  **kaṭavul** (கடவுள்) *'God'*

(134)  **kaṭṭu** (கட்டு) *'building'*

(135)  **kaṭṭu tuṟai** (கட்டுத் துறை) *'harbour'*

(136)  **kaṭu** (கடு) *'difficult'*

(137)  **kāvalan** (காவலன்)

(138)  ***kāvaṭi*** *(காவடி) yoke carried on shoulders with weights hung on both sides.*

(139)  **kay** (கை) 'hand'

(140)  **kay paṟṟuka** (கை பற்றுக) *'to hold hand as in wedlock'*

(141)  **kay paṟṟuka / piṭikka** (கை பற்றுக / பிடிக்க) *'to hold hand as in wedlock'*

(142)  **kīḻ** (கீழ்) **/ kiḻa** (கிழ)**;** ph.Syl.

(143)  **kiḻanku** (கிழங்கு) ***'pulp'***

(144)  **kī̲kunṟu** (கீழ்க்குன்று) *'Eastern Hill'*

(145)  **kiṇa** (கிண) **/ kē**(கே) **/ kī** (கீ); Ph.Syl.

(146)  **kiṇaṟu** (கிணறு) / **kēṇi** (கேணி)

(147)  **ko** (கொ); Ph.Syl.

(148)  **kō** (கோ) *'king'*

(149)  **kō** (கோ) *'king'*

(150)  **kodu** (கொடு) *'crest', 'summit'*

(151)  **koḷ** (கொள்) *'buy'*

(152) **kōl** (கோல்) *'pole, mast, stick, rod, sceptre'*

(153)  **kōl mīn** (கோல்மீன்) *'zodiac sign **libra'** துலாம் இராசி'*

(154)  **ko̲li** (கொழி) *'flourish'*

(155)  **kō̲li** (கோழி) *'fowl, hen'*

(156)  **kompan** (கொம்பன்) *'Tusked animal / Chieftan'*

(157)  **kompu** (கொம்பு)

(158)  **kompu** (கொம்பு) *'horn'*

(159)  **kōṇṭai** (கோண்டை)

(160)  **koṇṭai** (கொண்டை)

(161)  **koṭaiyāḷ** (கொடையாள்) *'Donor'*

(162)  **kōṭan** (கோடன் / கோடங்கி) *'diviner, sooth-sayer'*

(163)  **koṭṭai** (கொட்டை); *'nut'*

(164) 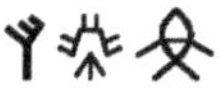 **koṭṭakai** (கொட்டகை) *'theatre'*

(165)  **kōṭṭay** (கோட்டை) *'temple', 'palace', 'fort'*

(166)  **koṭu** (கொடு) *'summit', 'mountain top'*

(167)  **koṭu** (கொடு) *'to give'.*

(168)  **kōṭu** (கோடு)

(169)  **kōṭu** (கோடு) *'horn'*

(170)  **kōvaṇam** (கோவணம்) *'male under-garment loin cloth'*

(171)  **kōvaṇam** (கோவணம்) *'man's under-garment loin cloth*

(172)  **ku** (கு); Ph.Syl.

(173)  **kū (கூ) / kō (கோ)**

(174)  **ku(கு) / ko(கொ)**

(175)  **kunṟu** (குன்று) *'hill, hillock'*

(176)  **kunṟu** (குன்று*)* *'hill, hillock'*

(177)  **kunti** (குந்தி)

(178)  **kuṟa /kuṟi / kuṟu** (குற /குறி / குறு) ***'short'***

(179)  **kuṟinci** (குறிஞ்சி) *'hilly area'*

(180)  **kuṟṟam (குற்றம்),** *'crime'*

(181)  **kūṭal** (கூடல்) ***'meeting-place'***

(182)  **kūṭam** (கூடம்) ***'crossroad'***

(183)  **kuṭi (குடி)** ***'to drink'***

(184)  **kuṭi (குடி, குலம்)** ***'social class'***

(185)  **kūttan** (கூத்தன்) *'actor, drama artist'*

(186)  **kūttanār** (கூத்தனார்) *actor, drama artist'*

(187)  **kūtti** (கூத்தி) *dancer, drama artiste'* (நடிகை, ஆட்டக்காரி)

(188)  **kuttu** (குத்து)

(189)  **kuttu** (குத்து)

(190)  **kuttu** (குத்து) *'to pound'*

(191)  **kūṭṭu** (கூட்டு) ***'joint'***

(192)  **kūttu (**கூத்து) *'dance, drama'*

(193)  **kūttu koṭṭakai** கூத்துக்கொட்டகை *'drama theatre'*

(194)  **kūṭu** (கூடு) *'nest'*

(195)  **kuvi** (குவி) *'converge'*

(196)  **kuviran** (குவிர) *'kuberan'*

(197)  **ḻi** (ழி); Ph. Syl.

(198)  **ḻu** (ழு); Ph. Syl.

(199)  **ma** (ம) **/ va** (வ)

(200)  **malai** (மலை) *'mount'; later form of* **varai**

(201)  **maḻai** (மழை) *'rain god',* (later on **varuṇa**)

(202)  **maḻai (**மழை) *'rain'*

(203)  **maḻai** (மழை) *'rain'*

(204)  **maḻai** (மழை) *'rain'*

(205) 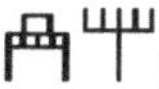 **māḷikai** (மாளிகை) *'Palace'*

(206)  **māḷikai ūr** (மாளிகை ஊர்)

(207)  **mān / makan** (மான் / மகன்) *'king, leader, man / son'*

(208)  **manṟam** (மன்றம்) **/ maṇṭapam** (மண்டபம்), *'public hall, memorial'*

(209)  **māri (**மாரி) *'deadly disease, small pox'*

(210)  **māri** (மாரி) *'rain'*

(211)  **māru** (மாறு) *'sell'*

(212)  **māṟu-koḷ-kūṭam** (மாறு-கொள்-கூடம்) ***'sell-buy-joint'***

(213)  **māṭam** (மாடம்) *'storeyed house'*

(214)  **māṭṭu** *(மாட்டு)* – '*for*', '*for the sake of*', '*on account of*

(215)  **māṭṭu** *(மாட்டு)* – 'to fasten on', 'to hook', 'hang', etc.

(216)  **māṭṭu** (மாட்டு) (post-position)

(217) ◇ **mē** (மே); ph.Syl.

(218) ◇ **mēl / mēn** (மேல் / மேன்)

(219)  **mēru** (மேரு) *'huge mountain range like Himalayas'*

(220) ◇ **mēṭu** (மேடு) *'top, raised platform, citadel'*

(221)  **mēṭu** (மேடு), *'citadel'*

(222)  **mīn mīnam (மீன் மீனம்) *'zodiac sign* pisces/**

(223)  ***mīṉ,*** (மீன்) 'fish', 'star'; *iconic value*

(224)  **mītu-poli** (மீது-பொலி) *'God's share of crop'*

(225)  **muḻu** (முழு) *'whole, entire'*

(226)  **mulu (முழு)** *'whole, entire'*

(227)  **munai, muni, nuni** (முனை, முனி, நுனி) ***'edge'***

(228)  **muni** (முனி) village deity

(229) U||| **mūṉṟām (mūnnām) kuṭi₂** *(மூன்றாம் - மூன்னாம்- குடி)*

(230)  **murukan** (முருகன்) *'Lord Muruga'*

(231)  **murukan** (முருகன்) *'Lord Muruga'*

(232)  **murukan** (முருகன்) *'Lord Muruga'*

(233) 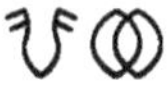 **murukan** (முருகன்) *'Lord Muruga';*

(234) 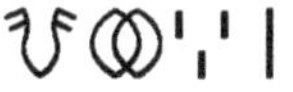 **murukan** (முருகன்) *"a person's name"*

(235)  **muruku** (முருகு)

(236)  **mutal kuṭi$_2$** *(முதல் குடி)*

(237)  **nā** (நா) / **ñā** (ஞா); ph. Syl.

(238)  **nakar** (நகர்)

(239)  **nakar** (நகர்) *'city, town'*

(240)  **nakar aincan** (நகர் ஐஞ்சன்) *'town panchayat member'*

(241)  **nakar āṭci** (நகராட்சி) (*town administration or Municipality)*

(242)  **nakar poṟaiyār** (நகர் பொறையார்) *'city mayor'*

(243)  **nal** (நல்) / **naṉ** (நன்); ph. Syl.

(244)  **naḷ (நள்) / naṇ (நண்);** ph. Syl.

(245)  **nāḷ** (நாள்) *'day'*

(246)  **nāḷ** (நாள்) *'day'*

(247)  **nal aiyai** (நல் ஐயை)

(248) 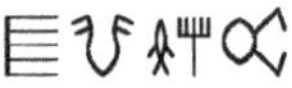 **nal aiyanār** (நல் ஐயனார்)

(249)  **nal iṟai pēṟikai** (நல் இறை பேரிகை) *'benevolent Royal Drum'*

(250)  **nāñcil / ñāñcil (**நாஞ்சில் / ஞாஞ்சில்) *'plough'*

(251)  **nānkām (nālām) kuṭi$_2$** *(நான்காம் - நாலாம்- குடி)*

(252)  **naṉṟu** (நன்று) *'well', good'*

(253)  **naṇṭu** (நண்டு) *'crab'*

(254)  **nāṟu** (நாறு) *'smell'*

(255)  **nāṭan** (நாடன்) *'mountain-country leader, forest-country leader'*  **naṭu (**நடு) *'mid'*

(256)  **nāṭu** (நாடு)

(257)  **nāṭu** (நாடு) *'country'*

(258)  **naṭukaḷ** (நடுகல்) *'Hero-stone'*

(259)  **naṭuvan (**நடுவன்) *'arbitrator', 'magistrate'.*

(260)  **naṭuvan** (நடுவன்) *'judge, arbitrator'*

(261)  **naṭuvar** (நடுவர்) *'Judge'*;

(262)  **naṭuvu** (நடுவு) *'middle'*

(263)  **nel** (நெல்) 'grain'

(264)  **nēr** (நேர்) *'straight'*

(265)  **neṭu / nīḷ / neṭum** (நெடு / நீள் / நெடும்) *'long, tall'*

(266)  **neṭuṅkunṟam** (நெடுங்குன்றம்); *place name*

(267)  **neṭuṅkunṟam** (நெடுங்குன்றம்); *place name*

(268)  **ṇi** (ணி); Ph.Syl.

(269)  **nuni / muni / munai,** (நுனி / முனி/ முனை) 'edge'

(270)  **o** (ஒ); *'o'* short vowel; ph. Syl.

(271)  **ō** (ஓ); *'ō'* long vowel; ph. Syl.

(272)  **ō** *long vowel;* ph. Syl.

(273)  **onpān** (ஒன்பான்) *'nine, ninefold'*; classical adjective form

(274)  **onpān** (ஒன்பான்) ***Navagraha,*** *a group of nine planets of Indian Astrology*

(275) **oru** (ஒரு) *'one'*

(276) **oru** (ஒரு) *'one'*

(277)  **ōtu** (ஓது) *'read, learn'*

(278)  **pa, pay / va, vay (**ப, பை / வ, வை**);**

Ph.Syl.

(279)  **pai** (நெல்) 'bag'

(280)  **paim / pasum** (பைம் / பசும்) 'green'

(281)  **pakal** (பகல்) *'daytime'*

(282)  **pakal** (பகல்) *'daytime'*

(283)  **pakavān** (பகவான்) *'Supreme Being'*

(284)  **pakavu** (பகவு) *'share'*

(285)  **pakirvu (**பகிர்வு**)** ***'share / sharing'***

(286)  **paku** (பகு) *'divide, distribute,share'*

(287)  **pakutaṟi vuṭai iṟaivan aṭi**

(பகுத்தறிவுடை இறைவன் அடி)

(288)  **pal** (பல்) 'tooth'

(289)  **pal** (பல்) 'tooth'

(290)  **pāl** (பால்) *'milk, white'*

(291)  **pāl** (பால்) *'milk, white'*

(292)  **pāḻi** (பாழி) *'town'* '

(293)  **pāḻi'** (பாழி)

(294)  **paḷḷi** (பள்ளி)

(295)  **paḷḷi** (பள்ளி) *village', hamlet'*

(296)  **pāṇan** (பாணன்) *'singer' I* **pulavan** (புலவன்) *'poet'*

(297)  **pāṇan** (*பெண்பால்* பாணன்)

(298)  **paṟṟi** (பற்றி) *'about', 'village', 'town'*

(299)  **paṟṟu** (பற்று) *'seize', 'hold', 'catch'*

(300)  **paṟṟu** (பற்று) *archaic form*; *'seize, catch, hold'*

(301)  **paṟṟu** (பற்று); *'seize, catch, hold'*

(302)  **paṭai** (*படை*) *'to offer / to perform pooja'*

(303)  **paṭai** (*படை*) *'to offer / to perform pooja'*

(304)  **paṭaiyal** (*படையல்*) *'offering / pooja'*

(305)  **paṭaiyal** (*படையல்*) *'offering / pooja'*

(306)  **paṭi** (படி), *'steps'*

(307)  **paṭi kaṭṭu** (படிக் கட்டு) *'Pond Steps'*

(308)  **paṭi tuṟai** (படித் துறை) *'swimming pool'*

(309)  **paṭṭi** (பட்டி) *'village', 'town'*

(310)  **paṭṭu** (பட்டு) *'silk', 'village', 'town'*

(311)  **paṭuvai** (படுவை) *'float'*

(312)  **paṭuvān** (படுவான்) 'west / sunset'

(313)  **payaṟu** (பயறு) *'pulse, grain'*

(314)  **payir** (பயிர்) 'crop'

(315)  **payir, nel, pay / pacum** (பயிர், நெல், பை / பசும்) 'crop, grain, bag / green'

(316)  **pe** (பெ), **pi** (பி), **pē** (பே), **pī** (பீ); Ph.Syl.

(317)  **pe** (பெ); ph. Syl.

(318)  **pē** (பே); ph. Syl.

(319)  **pēṇu** (பேணு) *'to rear, to take care'*

(320)  **pēṇu** **பேணு** (பேணி வளர்த்தல்) 'to rear children'

(321)  **pērikai** (பேரிகை) *'tom-tom, drum'*

(322)  **pērikai** (பேரிகை, முரசு) *'drum'*

(323)  **pērikai añcan** (பேரிகை அஞ்சன்) *'tom-tom messenger'*

(324)  **pērikai-ancan** (பேரிகை-அஞ்சன்) ***'drum announcer'***

(325)  **peṟu** (பெறு) *'to give birth, to receive'*

(326)  **pēṟu** (பேறு) *'boon'*

(327)  **peru / pēr / perum** (பெரு / பேர் / பெரும்) *'big, great'*

(328)  **peṟu** பெறு (அடைதல், பெறுதல்) 'to receive'

(329)  **peṟu** பெறு (குழந்தை பெறுதல்) 'to give birth'

(330)  **pēṟu** பேறு (பாக்கியம்) ''boon'

(331)  **perumān** *'king'*

(332)  **pi** (பி); ph. Syl.

(333)  **pī** (பீ); ph. Syl.

(334)  **piḻai (**பிழை**)** *'mistake' and also*

(335)  **piṟa** (பிற) *'to be born'*

(336)  **piṟa** பிற (குழந்தையாகப் பிறத்தல்) 'to be born'

(337)  **poṟai** *(பொறை)* – 'bearer', 'official'

(338)  **poṟai** (பொறை) *''person-in-charge, official'*

(339)  **poṟai** *(பொறை), responsibility*

(340)  **poṟaiyan** (பொறையன்)

(341)  **poṟaiyan** *(பொறையன்)* – 'bearer', 'official'

(342) 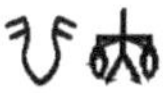 **poṟaiyan** (பொறையன்) *'officer'*

(343)  **poṟaiyanār** (பொறையனார்) 'administrator'

(344)  **poṟu** *(பொறு)* - 'to bear', 'to sustain'.

(345)  **poti** *(பொதி)*, load, burden, responsibility,

(346)  **potiyan** (பொதியன்)

(347)  **ppa** (ப்ப)

(348)  **ppā (**ப்பா)

(349)  **pū** (பூ) *'flower'*

(350)  **puṟam** (புறம், வெளி) *'outside'*

(351)  **puṟam** (புறம், வெளி) *'outside'*

(352)  **ri** (றி); ph.Syl.

(353)  **<u>ṟṟ</u>** (ற்ற) archaic form; Ph.Syl.

(354)  **<u>ṟṟ</u>** (ற்ற); Ph.Syl.

(355)  **ṟu** (று); Ph. Syl.

(356)  **sa (**ஸ**);** dental sibilant Ph.Syl.

(357)  **savayan** (சவையன்) ***'academician'***

(358)  **su / si** (ஸு / ஸி); ph.Syl.

(359)  **ta (**த) dental plosive Ph.Syl.

(360)  **ta / sa** (த / ஸ); ph.Syl.

(361)  **takayan (**தகையன்) *'aristocrat / owner'*

(362)  **talai** (தலை) *'head'*

(363)  **talai** (தலை) *'head'*

(364)  **tāḻi** (தாழி) *'urn'*

(365)  **tāṅku** *(தாங்கு)* – 'to bear', 'to hold'

(366)  **tappan** (தப்பன்) *'drummer'*

(367)  **tappu** (தப்பு) *'drum'*

(368)  **tappu** (தப்பு) *'fault'*

(369)  **taṟi (தறி)** ***'stake'***

(370)  **taṟi** *(***தறி**) and *phonetic syllable* **ta / sa** (த / ஸ)

(371)  **tavaṟu** (**தவறு**) *'wrong',*

(372)  **tēn** (தேன்) *'honey'*

(373)  **tompai / tumpai** (தொம்பை / தும்பை) *'granary / shrub'*

(374)  **toṭu / paṭu (**தொடு / படு), *'touch'*

(375)  **toṭuvān** (தொடுவான்) 'east / horizon'

(376)  **ṭṭ** (ட்ட)**;** Ph. Syl.

(377)  **tu (**து) / **to (**தொ)

(378)  **tū (**தூ) / **tō (**தோ)

(379)  **tu / to** (து / தொ); ph.Syl.

(380)  **ṭu** or **ḍu** (-டு); ph.Syl.

(381)  **tūkku** *(தூக்கு)* – 'to lift'

(382)  **tumpai mēṭu** (தும்பை மேடு)

(383)  **tumpaimēdu** (தும்பைமேடு)

(384)  **tūṇ** தூண் ***'pillar'***

(385)  **tuṇai** துணை ***'support'***

(386)  **tuṟai** (துறை) *'port, harbour'*

(387)  **tuvarai** (துவரை); Harappan name for the city-state **dvārakā** (*<u>Dwaraka)</u>*

(388)  **u** (உ); *'u'* short vowel; ph. Syl.

(389)  **u** or **ū** *vowel;* ph. Syl.

(390)  **uaccan** (உவச்சன்) *'priest'*

(391)  **uḷ** (உள்) *'inside'* locative grammatical particle

(392)  **ulam** (உலம்) *'pestle'*

(393)  **ulam** (உலம், உலக்கை) 'pestle'

(394)  **ulamkalam** (உலங்கலம்) *'pestle and mortar'*

(395)  **un, ūn, uṇ, ūṇ** (உன், ஊன், உண், ஊண்); Ph.Syl.

(396)  **ūr** (ஊர்) *'town'*

(397)  **ū**r (ஊர்) *'town', 'village'*

(398)  **ūr** (ஊர்) *'town',*

(399)  **uṟai** (உறை) 'residence'

(400) 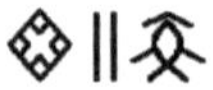 **uṟaiyūr / oṟaiyūr** (உறையூர் / ஒறையூர்)

(401) 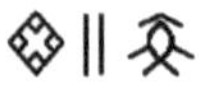 **uṟaiyūr** (உறையூர்); name of a place

(402)  **ural** (உரல்) *'pestle and mortar / grinder'*

(403)  **ural** (உரல்) *'pestle and mortar'*

(404)  **uṟu** (உறு) 'appropriate'

(405)  **usakayan** (உசக்கையன்) *'counsellor'*

(406)  **uṭai** (உடை)

(407) 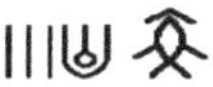 **uṭai** (உடை) *'break'*

(408)  **uṭai** (உடை) *'possession, dress'*

(409)  **uṭu** (உடு) 'wear, star'

(410)  **vai / mai** (வை / மை) *word ending*

(411)  **vaḷ** (வல்) 'strength'

(412)  **vāḻ** (வாழ்) *'to live'*

(413)  **vāḻ** (வாழ்) *to live'*

(414)  **vāḷ (வாள்)** ***'sword'***

(415)  **vāḻappan** (வாழப்பன்) / **vāḻvappan** (வாழ்வப்பன்)

(416)  **vaḷḷal** (வள்ளல்) *'philanthropist*

(417)  **vaḻu (வழு)** *'error',*

(418) 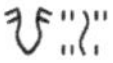 **vāḻvan** (வாழ்வன்) *'living person'*

(419)  ***vaṇikar*** (வணிகர்)

(420)  **vāṇiyar** (வாணியர்) or **vaṇikar** (வணிகர்)

(421)  **vān-kaṭavul** (வான்-கடவுள்) *'Celestial God'*

(422)  **vānku** (வாங்கு) *'receive'*

(423)  **varai** (வரை) *'mountain'*

(424)  **vāy** (வாய்) *'mouth'*

(425)  **vēlan** (வேலன்)

(426)  **vēlappan** (வேலப்பன்)

(427)  ***vēḷar*** (வேளர்)

(428)  **veḷar** (வேளர்) or **veḷāḷar** (வேளாளர்)

(429) 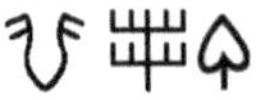 **vēlayyan** (வேலய்யன்)

(430)  **veḷiccam** வெளிச்சம் ***'light'***

(431)  **veṟiyāṭu** (வெறியாடு) *'dance in trance under possession by Muruga'*

(432)  **veyil** (வெயில்) ***'sunshine'***

(433)  **veyil / vēnal** (வெயில் / வேனல்) *'sun's heat'*

(434)  **vī / vē** (வீ / வே) *'bird'*

(435)  **viri (விரி)** *'diverge*

(436)  **vīṭu** (வீடு)

(437)  **vu** (வு)

(438)  **yāḻ** (யாழ்) *'ancient musical instrument'*, **pāṇ** (பாண்) *'song, poem'*

(439)  **yēṇi** (யேணி) / **ēṇi** (ஏணி) *'ladder'*

www.ingramcontent.com/pod-product-compliance
Lightning Source LLC
LaVergne TN
LVHW061612070526
838199LV00078B/7249
9789359890630